Learn to Play Guitar WITH 8 CHORDS

By Stephen Dydo

ISBN 1-57560-594-5

Visit our website at www.cherrylane.com

INTRODUCTION: HOW TO USE THIS BOOK

Why Eight Chords?

I've put together this book to show the beginning or early intermediate guitarist how to play a lot of songs with a minimum of memorization. Eight chords are all you'll need to play every song in this book, as well as a lot of other songs in a lot of other books. You'll see some basic strumming patterns that are effective in these songs as well. So if you've never played a guitar before, this is a good place to start. And if you've been playing a while, this will help you to organize what you know, and maybe even teach you a few things about what you've already been doing.

The organization of the book is based on the introduction of the eight chords in a gradual fashion, with songs following each new chord. Along the way, I introduce different strums as appropriate for the new songs. Often, a new strum can be useful for earlier songs as well. You may be amazed at how many songs you can play with only eight chords, and we only scratch the surface in this book.

But how can you play so many songs with only eight chords? There are a lot of guitar chords out there, certainly more than a thousand. This is a potentially daunting statistic. Please don't let it daunt you! Would you like to hazard a guess as to how many guitarists use all of them? Try the number "0"—it's likely the right one. Why should that be the case, since it is certainly possible to learn all of them, given enough time? Well, every chord has a different sound, a different playing position, and a different useful context. For example, the lead guitarist and the rhythm guitarist might both play a chord with the same name, but it's unlikely that they'll play it in the same way. They're each trying to create a different sound, and the way they each finger the chord is part of that sound.

Who is this Book for?

In principle, I've provided enough information so that someone who has never played the guitar will be able to start right here. The basics of how to hold the guitar, how to tune it, how to read the chord frames, and so forth are covered. If you have been playing for a while, feel free to cheerfully skip these parts, although it's often interesting to review even the most basic points.

This can also serve as a songbook for those who have already mastered all of the chords and playing techniques presented. The selection of songs will be most familiar to an adult audience, so you can think of this as a tutorial songbook for folks who have finished school—but you don't need a college degree to get through it!

A word about the notation: Although I've included the notes of the songs written out in staff notation, you don't have to be able to read it. All guitar music is written out in simple symbols above the staff that will be explained soon.

Do I Need a Teacher?

Although you can definitely use this book to teach yourself the basics of chords and strumming on your own, the answer to this is "yes, always," no matter how long you've been playing the guitar. The main reason for this is that it's always beneficial to have someone with experience looking at your playing style. This can go from having a weekly lesson with lots of homework to chatting with another player on the road who points out an easier way to do a chord change. Beginner or professional, you can always learn from others.

Of course, in the earlier stages of learning to play, one is much more in need of advice than later on. So if you can use this book with a teacher, it'll go that much better. But if you haven't got one at the moment, this will help you out with the basics at the beginning and some of the tricky bits later on. If you've already mastered some of the learning material presented here, feel free to skip over it; but it may give you a new and helpful slant on some things you've been doing for a while.

■ *A Note for Lefties*

The text in this book describes how a right-handed person plays the guitar. This is for convenience only! There are many excellent left-handed guitarists, and if you're planning to become one of them, please don't be put off by this text convention. Assuming that you play with your right hand on the fretboard and your left hand over the body of the guitar, all of the diagrams and photos will be reversed for you, as well as all references to the right and left hands.

■ THE BASICS

■ *What Kind of Guitar Do I Need?*

The songs in this book are geared towards acoustic guitar performance. However, all of the techniques described are applicable to the electric guitar as well. So, whether you're working with a steel-string acoustic, a nylon-string folk guitar, an electric, or a classical, there is plenty of material for you here.

■ *How to Select a Guitar*

The first three things to do before getting your guitar are:

• Decide what type of guitar you want. (You probably made that decision when you heard the guitarist that first made you want to learn to play, but it wouldn't hurt to rethink it.)

• Figure out your budget for the instrument. There aren't really any guidelines for this; sometimes you can get a good deal from a tag sale for under $100, but you need to know what you're doing. And remember that there are instruments out there for more than $10,000; the price range is huge.

• If you don't have a lot of experience, be sure that you have someone who does check out the guitar for you. Getting a guitar is not like getting married. You might end up playing the instrument for thirty years or more, but it's a relatively simple matter to decide at any time that you made a mistake or you want something more.

■ *Another Note for Lefties*

Left-handed players do have to deal with an issue that righties don't—almost all guitars are made for right-handed players. The extent to which this is an issue depends on your solution to the problem, which can be one of the following.

• Get a guitar made for left-handed players. Then, you will use your right hand for fingering the chords and your left hand for strumming and picking. This has the advantage of sound (the guitar is built to be played this way) and technique (you use the favored hand the same way right-handed players do). The disadvantages are that you won't have a lot of selection unless you're getting a guitar custom built (nice, but expensive), and that the illustrations and chord frames will be reversed for you.

• Get a guitar that you like and, assuming it's built for righties, reverse the stringing and see if you still like it. (A reasonable return policy is important here. Also, unless you have some familiarity with guitar set-up, you'll need the assistance of someone who does.) Obviously, this is only an option for guitars with symmetrical bodies. Assuming that the guitar has fret-position dots on the side of the neck, either get one with the dots on both sides (albeit this is uncommon), or have a *luthier* (a person who builds and repairs guitars and several other kinds of stringed instruments) place dots for you on the opposite side, which shouldn't be very expensive. The advantages are that the technique is the same as for right-handed players, and that the availability of guitars, or at least reasonably priced ones, is better. The disadvantages are that you are restricted to an instrument with a symmetrical body, you have to restring it to see if the sound will work, and you may have to modify the instrument to a greater or lesser degree. Also, as above, the illustrations and chord frames here will be reversed for you.

- Play a right-handed guitar the way righties do, with your right hand over the body and your left hand on the neck. Whether this is an option or not will depend on your degree of ambidexterity. If this works for you, you have all advantages and no disadvantages. (I know a right-handed player who uses her left hand for strumming and her right hand for fingering the chords, so it's certainly a possibility.)

- Play a right-handed guitar with your left hand over the body and your right hand on the neck, and don't modify the guitar. This means that you will have a special fretting technique, and some strums will not work the same way as they do for righties. For one thing, when you do a downstroke with your hand or pick, the strings of the chord will sound in the reverse order of the same stroke by a righty. Generally, this is not recommended, but at least one truly excellent guitarist has played this way.

■ *How to Hold the Guitar*

There are two ways to hold the guitar: sitting down and standing. If you're standing, you should have a strap on your guitar. Whichever way you do it, don't be afraid to shift your position a bit to find the most relaxing position.

Sitting

Your best seat is on a chair with no arms. A couch can do in a pinch, but it's not optimal. The chair should be high enough so that your feet are flat on the ground and your legs are more or less straight. The waist (the narrowest part of the guitar body) should rest on your right leg, with the back of the guitar against your body. (If your guitar is not built along the traditional hourglass lines, then you should probably stand).

Standing

The strap should hold the guitar at a height such that your hand is over the strings when your arm is just about parallel with the ground. Please don't play standing without a strap for any length of time; it's too easy to build up tension in your arms by supporting the guitar, and then comes tendonitis, etc. Normally, the neck of the guitar is angled up a bit.

■ *The Notes of the Guitar*

First off, let's clear up a bit of terminology: When I speak of the highest string of the guitar, I'm talking about the thinnest one that is normally closest to the ground (that is, physically, the lowest string). When I talk about the lowest string, I mean the thickest one that is furthest from the ground. "Low" and "high" refer to pitch, not physical location.

Now that we've cleared that up, the notes of the six *open* (not fretted—your left-hand fingers aren't involved) strings, from the lowest to the highest, are E–A–D–G–B–E. Without going into details, let's say that the pitch of high (thinnest) string is an E two octaves above the low (thickest) E. Written in staff notation, for those interested, the notes are as follows.

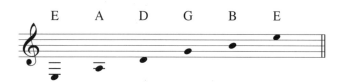

How to Tune the Guitar

The most reliable way to tune a guitar, at least until you've got the sounds of the notes of the guitar solidly into your ears, is to use an electronic tuner. These devices can listen to you play a note on the guitar and then not only tell you which note it is, but tell you whether it's too high, too low, or just right. There are two types you can use. One is specifically made for guitars and can give a reading for the specific strings of the guitar. The other is generic and just tells you what you've played into it. Get the guitar-specific kind unless you think that you might use it for tuning other instruments, and follow the manufacturer's directions to tune your guitar.

If you don't have a tuner and don't want to buy one, never fear—you can still tune your guitar, or at least adjust the strings so that they are in tune with each other.

If at all possible, first tune either the low E or the A string to a sound source such as another guitar (tune your low E string to match someone else's), a piano, a pitch pipe, or a tuning fork (tuning forks are generally pitched to A, so tune your A string to match). Since most A tuning forks are tuned to a pitch two octaves higher than the A string (in other words, it's the same note, only in a higher scale—it is even called the same thing, an A), you should tune two octaves lower. Once that is set, do not change that string's tuning any more.

You can tune the strings to each other with the following method. First, place a left-hand finger on the low E string at the 5th fret (right behind what's called the *fret wire* at the 5th fret—apply pressure and *voilà*) and play the note with a right-hand finger or a pick. The note you play should sound the same as the open (not fretted—just played like it is) A string. If it isn't, here's what you should do: if you originally tuned the low E string to a sound source, then adjust the A string up or down to match it in pitch, but if you tuned the A string to a sound source instead, tune the E string up or down until its pitch is the same as the A. (If you're tuning the E to the A, you'll need to remove your finger from the E string, adjust the pitch, and then put the finger back just behind that 5th fret and play the string to check it—repeat as necessary.) Then go through the same process tuning the open D string to the 5th fret note on the A string, the open G string to the 5th fret note on the D string, the open B to the 4th (that's right, *not* the 5th) fret note on the G string, and finally the open high E string to the 5th fret note on the B string. Other than the 4th fret on the G string, you will always tune a string to the next lower string at the 5th fret.

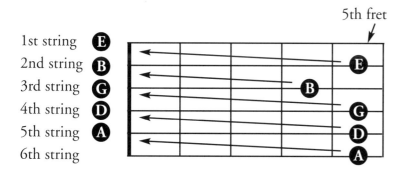

How to "Read" the Music in This Book

For each song in this book, you'll be given four pieces of important musical information at once. From bottom to top, these are: melody notes on a standard musical *staff* (that collection of five horizontal lines upon which notes are planted), rhythmic notation (often referred to in the guitar world as "rhythm slashes"), chord frames, and chord names. It all looks like this.

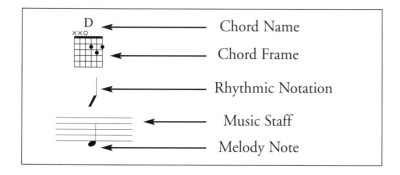

Let's start with the bottom part: melody notes on a standard musical staff. Since the full story on how to read music is a bit beyond the scope of this book, think of these melody notes (which will be accompanied by lyrics immediately below in the songs) as "reminders" as to what the *pitches* (notes) in the song are doing. If you already know how to read music, then these melody notes will be meaningful to you. But if you don't know how to read music, never fear—you already know most, if not all, of the songs in this book anyway! Also, here's a hint until you've digested everything this book has to offer and have decided to take your playing to the next level: the higher on the staff, the higher the pitch of the note, the lower on the staff, the lower the pitch of the note.

Second from the bottom, right above the music staff, are the *rhythm slashes*. These tell you when to strum a chord, and how long you should *hold* that chord (that is, how long it should ring out before you play another one, or even just let the song end). For those of you who are familiar with reading notes on a staff, these are a no-brainer, as they look just like standard notes (they mean the same things rhythmically, too), except their noteheads are "squared-off," and not round. Each rhythm slash stands for a certain number of beats, and everything is based on a beat called a *quarter note*. Below is a chart that describes the different kinds of rhythm slashes that you'll find in this book. Note that a dot right after a slash means that its value is increased by one-half of that slash's value.

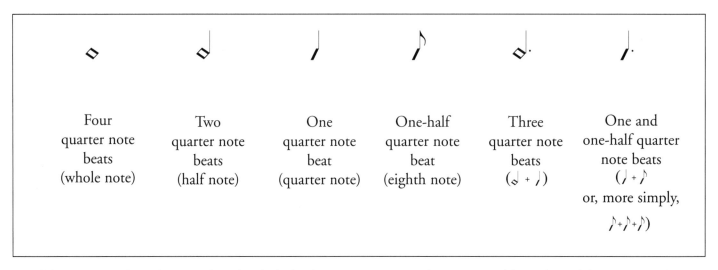

| Four quarter note beats (whole note) | Two quarter note beats (half note) | One quarter note beat (quarter note) | One-half quarter note beat (eighth note) | Three quarter note beats | One and one-half quarter note beats |

You'll learn more about beats and such a little bit later. For now, just keep in mind how the subdivisions work.

The third element from the bottom is what's called a *chord frame*. This is a really important "helper" if you're just learning how to play guitar, as it will tell you *how* you play each chord. You won't even have to turn back in the book if you've forgotten anything—the reminder will be right there! We'll go over what the different parts of the chord frame mean in just little bit.

And, last but not least, that letter on the top is the name of the chord.

■ *How to Read a Time Signature*

First of all, here's what a time signature looks like.

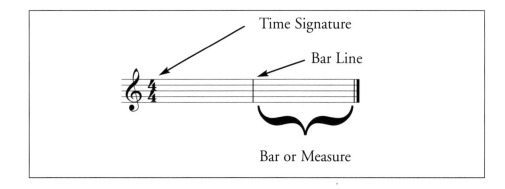

The bottom number refers to the type of note that is used for the basic beat. An "8" means an eighth note is used, "4" means a quarter note is used, "2" means a half note, and "1" means a whole note. The top number indicates the number of these kinds of notes that make up each *measure* or *bar* (same thing). Each measure is delineated by a *barline*.

So, in the time signature above, called "four-four," the basic beat is a quarter note, and there are four quarter notes per measure. (By the way, the first beat of a group is always *accented,* or played just a little more loudly than the notes that fall after it in the grouping). This rhythmic background of a piece is also called the *meter.*

Think of all of the beats as regular background ticks—and by "background," I mean that these ticks are not necessarily *heard* (although they can be), but they are always *felt.* For instance, if a piece is in "four-four", there will be a regular background "feel" of " *1–2–3–4, 1–2–3–4*" or more simply, " *bom*–bom–bom–bom, *bom*–bom–bom–bom". This might not have much to do with the actual sound of the song—that is, this underlying pattern might support a rhythm that skips some of the beats and adds notes in between others—but this is normal.

Now, on to the music! But first . . . your first chord!

INTRODUCING THE D CHORD

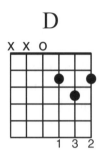

There are a lot of different ways to play a D chord. The one in this book is sometimes called the *open* D. This is because it uses a lot of open strings—only three of the strings are stopped with left hand fingers.

But wait—what does the information in the diagram *mean* and how do you *play* the chord?

How to Read a Chord Frame

If this is the first time you've played chords on the guitar, there are definitely a few things you should pay attention to. If this is old-hat to you, you can blissfully skip this section.

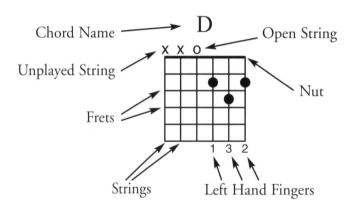

This is a chord frame. It is a diagram showing how to place the fingers of the left hand on the neck of the guitar to play a particular chord, as well as whether or not certain strings are picked or strummed with the right hand. This is how the chord frame should be interpreted.

- The vertical lines indicate the strings. The left-most vertical line represents the low E string, while the right-most represents the high E string. (Remember, when we talk about low and high in "guitar talk," we mean low-sounding and high-sounding—we're not referring to physical position when you're sitting to play.)

- The horizontal lines indicate the frets on the guitar. The frets are the metal strips that run crosswise on the neck of the guitar. The strip at the very top of the guitar neck, just before you get to the *headstock* (where the tuning machines live and the strings are anchored) is called the *nut*.

- The black dots show where a left-hand finger is placed behind a fret. By behind, I mean the position just to the left of the fret such that the string is able to vibrate freely just to the right of the fret. A note that is produced in this way is called a *fretted* note.

- An "o" indicates that the string below it is to be played *open*—that is, the entire string vibrates freely, without being fretted by any left-hand fingers.

- An "x" indicates a string that is not part of the chord at all, and is not to be played (strummed, picked, etc.) by the right hand.

- The numbers indicate which fingers are to be used to fret the strings. "1" indicates your index finger, "2" indicates your middle finger, "3" indicates your ring finger, and "4" indicates your pinky. Note that the particular fingers used are not normally indicated in a chord frame in an actual piece of music, but they are included in this book when a chord is first being taught.

Here is the standard way of fretting the D chord shown above:

To play the chord, you have to fret the notes and then strum the guitar. For this first strum, just use your thumb. Starting on the 4th string (remember: leave the 6th and 5th ones out because of the "x"s), draw it down across the strings in a smooth manner. Listen to each string—is it sounding properly? If it isn't, check to see if there is a finger touching it that shouldn't be; and if it's a fretted note, check your fingers and finger pressure and adjust accordingly.

Got that? Ready for another one?

INTRODUCING THE A CHORD

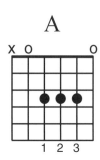

A

Try fretting and strumming this chord with your thumb until you feel comfortable with the sound and feel.

■ *Strumming with the Fingers—A Basic 3/4 Strum*

This first strumming pattern is in 3/4 (take a look at the time signature at the beginning of the music). What is this 3/4 meter? For our purposes, it means that this song is rhythmically organized into groups of three beats, with each beat indicated by a quarter note. If you're familiar with waltzes, they're a great example of this type of rhythmic structure. The basic underlying pulse of such a song is:

1-2-3, 1-2-3, 1-2-3, 1-2-3, etc.

The actual strumming technique to use here involves a downward stroke of the right hand. The fingernails should lightly brush all of the strings (except the ones marked with "x"s on the chord frame) in a quick, even stroke. Try strumming the "*1-2-3*" pattern a few times. Be careful about the "return"—it should *not* touch the strings; it just returns the hand to position for the next downstroke. On the first beat of a group, use a little more force than with the others—this will give the proper accent.

By the way, any good strumming technique is based on a *loose* right hand. "Limp as a dishrag" might be a good way to think of it. It should feel as if the fingers themselves are being tossed down by the hand, and brush the strings along the way.

"(Oh, My Darling) Clementine"

This is an old American folk song. The simplicity of the musical setting is a backdrop for the tragicomic stream of Verses. The Chorus should be strong, if not raucous. Use the basic 3/4 strum you just learned.

Do you see at the beginning and end of the music those thick and thin barlines with the dots? Those are *repeat signs,* and they tell you that the music between them is to be repeated (in this case, until you run out of Verses). When you see one of these signs with its dots on the right, it's the beginning of the repeated section (where you go back to), and when the dots are on the left, it's the end of the repeated section (where you jump back from). Those brackets at the end of the song with the "1.2.3." and then the "4." indicate which endings you should use for Verses 1, 2, 3, and 4, respectively. That thick and thin barline without the dots under the "4" bracket indicates that this is the end of the song.

Words and Music by
Percy Montrose

2. Light she was and like a fairy,
    And her shoes were number nine;
    Herring boxes, without topses,
    Sandals were for Clementine. *(To Chorus)*

3. Drove she ducklings to the water,
    Every morning just at nine;
    Hit her foot against a splinter,
    Fell into the foaming brine. *(To Chorus)*

4. Ruby lips above the water,
    Blowing bubbles, soft and fine;
    But Alas! I was no swimmer,
    So I lost my Clementine. *(To Chorus)*

Did you notice the little marks right above the rhythm slashes in the first full measure? Those indicate that the strums are *downstrums* (the down-only strum you've just learned). You'll learn about another mark a little later on.

■ *Strumming with a Pick*

Using a pick is the most common way of strumming. When you have a relaxed right hand technique, it's very easy to add a pick. Holding it is quite natural, and you don't need to hold it tightly.

Now try to play "Clementine" the same way as before, only with the pick. The basic strum is really almost the same as without a pick—the basic principles are the same. The main differences are that the right arm is usually held a bit straighter, and, since the pick is doing the actual sound production instead of your fingers, there's a bit less wrist action. As before with the fingers, the pick should lightly brush the strings.

How do you find out how tightly to hold the pick? Play with a relatively tight grip for a few bars, then loosen it a tiny bit. Is the pick secure? Then try a few bars with the grip loosened a bit more. Repeat until the pick is knocked out of position, then put it back into position and try a very slightly firmer grip. The goal is to go back and forth above and below the critical "point of departure" for the pick to determine the least amount of pressure required to hold it in place. Once you've found it, try to prevent yourself from using a firmer grip. Until you're really secure in this knowledge, go through the grip test every time you begin a practice session.

Strumming with just your hand is an excellent technique, and you'll probably keep using it—especially when you've lost your pick! But you'll find that, with a pick, you'll be able to get a brighter tone.

Note: If your guitar does not have a *pick guard* (usually, a piece of sheet plastic attached to the body of the guitar around the strumming area), you should be especially careful with the pick. If it's a good classical guitar, you may want to consider sticking with bare-hand strumming.

INTRODUCING THE E CHORD

E

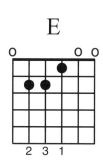

The high and low E strings in this chord ring out quite a lot. Often, you'll find that you have to hold back a bit with this one to prevent other chords in a song from getting overwhelmed.

"Rock-a-Bye, Baby"

This is certainly one of the best-known songs in America, sung not only by mothers to their infants, but also, with a different intent, by cartoon characters such as Bugs Bunny. The tune itself is actually far from the easiest to sing, so give yourself a little practice with the melody before you start to accompany yourself with the guitar.

Although the strum pattern here is the same as for "Clementine," the feel must be quite different. "Clementine" is raucous and funny. "Rock-a-bye Baby," even if done for humorous effect, should be gentle. As you get comfortable playing through the chords, keep the idea of a rocking boat in your image of the music.

This next group of songs contains all three of the chords you've learned so far. This is a great opportunity for review. Make sure the transitions from one chord to the next are really clean. One way to do this is to practice the *changes* (transitions from one chord to another) by themselves. Fret and play the first chord once, and then set up your fingers for the next one. When they're all in place, play the chord. Don't play anything with the right hand until you're sure the left hand is ready. Eventually, you should be able to play with a steady (even if slow) pulse, with a smooth connection between each pair of chords. You may take a while getting to this point, but it's the most efficient way to learn.

"On Top of Old Smoky"

This is the classic Appalachian love ballad, full of angst and yet, perhaps because of endless caricatures ("On Top of Spaghetti," etc.—you probably know others as well), or something inherent in the original, full of comic overtones to our modern ears. Whether you do it "straight" or with some humor, the accompaniment should be simple. Use the basic 3/4 strum, and don't overdo it.

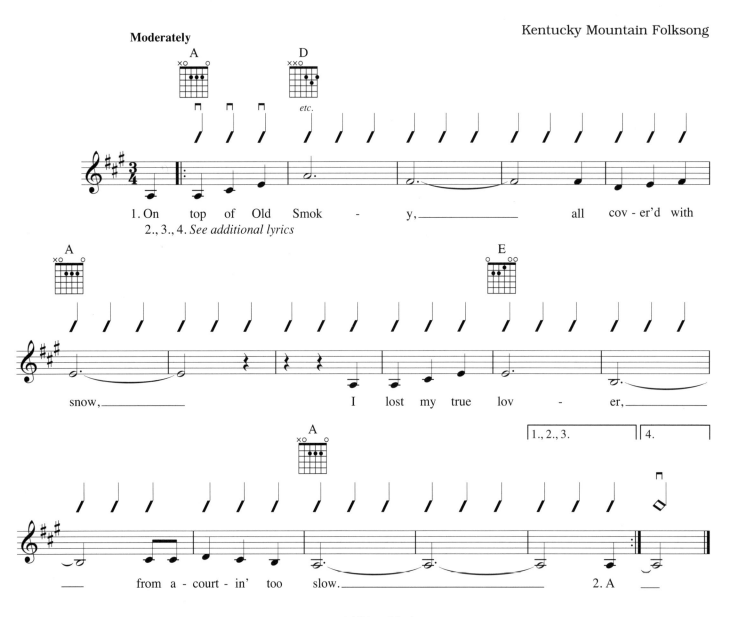

Kentucky Mountain Folksong

1. On top of Old Smok - y, _____ all cov - er'd with
2., 3., 4. *See additional lyrics*

snow, _____ I lost my true lov - er, ____

____ from a - court - in' too slow. _____ 2. A ___

Additional Lyrics

2. A courting's a pleasure,
   A courting's a grief,
   A false-hearted lover
   Is worse than a thief.

3. A thief he will rob you
   And take what you have,
   A false hearted lover
   Will send you to your grave.

4. The grave will decay you
   And turn you to dust,
   Not one boy in a hundred
   A poor girl can trust.

"Amazing Grace"

This beloved melody can be found in many old American hymnbooks. Because of its elegant simplicity, it has been used in many contexts outside of religion, but it always retains a certain homespun majesty. This melody is also in 3/4, but you're going to add a little bit to the basic strum. On the second half of the third beat, do an added strum with the pick. So, instead of strumming a simple " *1-2-3, 1-2-3*" you'll now do " *1-2-3-and, 1-2-3-and.*" The "3-and" strums are twice as fast (or half as long, depending on your point of view) than the " *1-2*" strums. Try it out on just an A chord before you play the song, and when you've got the feel down, dive right in.

Words by John Newton
from A Collection of Sacred Ballads
Traditional American Melody
from Carrell and Clayton's Virginia Harmony
Arranged by Edwin O. Excell

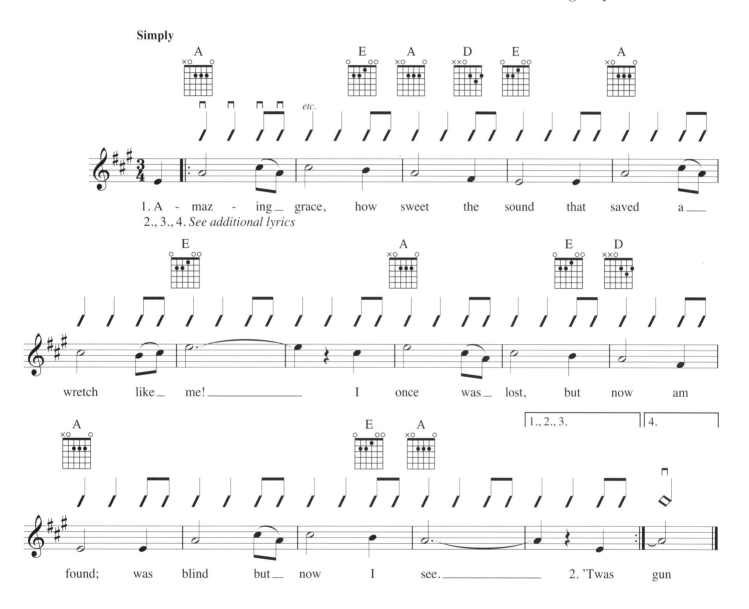

Additional Lyrics

2. 'Twas grace that taught my heart to fear,
   And grace my fears relieved,
   How precious did that grace appear
   The hour I first believed.

3. Through many dangers, toils, and snares,
   I have already come.
   'Tis grace that brought me safe thus far,
   And grace will lead me home.

4. When we've been there ten thousand years,
   Bright shining as the sun,
   We've no less days to sing God's praise,
   Than when we first begun.

"Old Macdonald Had a Farm"

This song is in 4/4, which means that the basic background feel is "*1-2-3-4, 1-2-3-4,*" or four strums to each measure. Keep your downstrums nice and even.

Traditional

Additional Lyrics

2. Old Macdonald had a farm,
    E-I-E-I-O!
    And on his farm he had some ducks,
    E-I-E-I-O!
    With a quack-quack here, and a quack-quack there,
    Here a quack, there a quack, everywhere a quack-quack.
    Old Macdonald had a farm,
    E-I-E-I-O!

3. Old Macdonald had a farm,
    E-I-E-I-O!
    And on his farm he had some cows,
    E-I-E-I-O!
    With a moo-moo here, and a moo-moo there,
    Here a moo, there a moo, everywhere a moo-moo.
    Old Macdonald had a farm,
    E-I-E-I-O!

4. Old Macdonald had a farm,
    E-I-E-I-O!
    And on his farm he had some pigs,
    E-I-E-I-O!
    With an oink-oink here, and an oink-oink there,
    Here an oink, there an oink, everywhere an oink-oink.
    Old Macdonald had a farm,
    E-I-E-I-O!

"Kumbaya"

Now let's try putting an extra strum on the last beat again. Just like "Old Macdonald," this song is in 4/4, which means that the basic background feel is "*1-2-3-4, 1-2-3-4*," but here you should strum "*1-2-3-4-and, 1-2-3-4-and*." Try this out on just a D chord until you feel confident and then try playing the song.

Traditional Spiritual

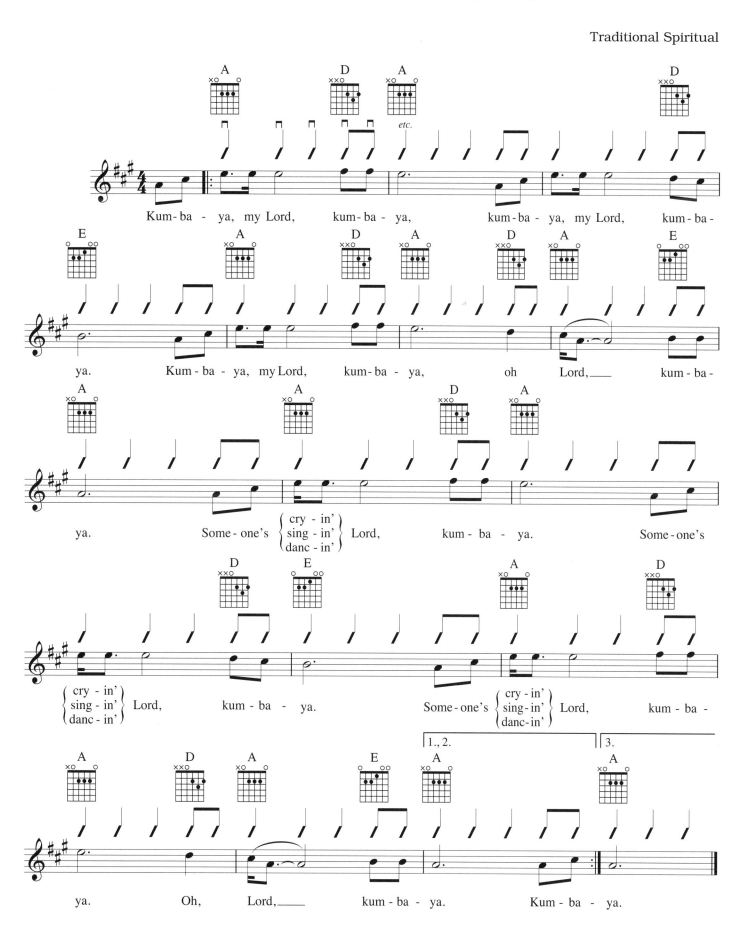

INTRODUCING THE G CHORD

The G chord can be played with more variant fingerings than almost any other. The one here is an *open* G—that is, it uses the most open strings possible for the chord.

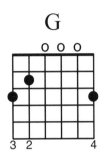

G

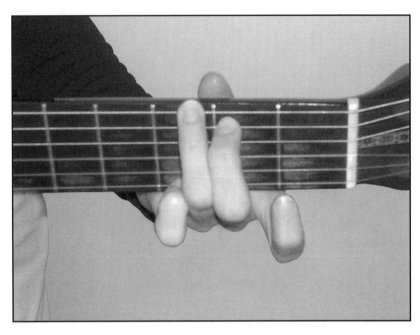

■ *The Down-Up Strum*

Up until this point we have been working entirely with downstrokes in our strum patterns. Now it's time to add the upstroke. On the upstrum, brush the strings in the reverse direction. This should have less of an accent than the downstroke, and it should be *light*. There will be occasions when you'll want to use a powerful upstroke as well, but for starting out, it's best to have an "unaccented" one. This is partly because that's the way musical rhythms generally work.

An upstroke often can take in fewer strings than the downstroke. For example, while playing an A chord, you can play all strings on the downstroke, and just play the upper three or four strings on the upstroke, if you'd like.

"Silent Night"

Few melodies have as romantic an origin as this classic Christmas carol. It was composed by musician-schoolteacher Franz Gruber in the Austrian village of Arnsdorf. On Christmas Eve of 1818, his friend Joseph Mohr, pastor of a nearby church, visited Gruber. He brought along with him a poem that he himself had written. He asked Gruber if he could set the poem to a new melody, with guitar accompaniment. Gruber, clearly nothing if not a working musician, set about the task eagerly. The piece was performed by the church choir at that evening's Midnight Mass. The guitar part of the original would have been a classical setting, which we won't try to duplicate here. The necessary gentle quality should come from a smooth connection from stroke to stroke. The key qualities to aim for are gentleness, smoothness, and fullness of tone.

By the way, that little "v" shape over the second note is the symbol for an upstroke.

Words by Joseph Mohr
Translated by John F. Young
Music by Franz X. Gruber

1. Si - lent night! Ho - ly night! All is
2., 3. *See additional lyrics*

calm, all is bright. Round yon Vir - gin

Moth - er and Child! Ho - ly In - fant so ten - der and

mild, sleep in heav - en - ly peace!

Sleep in heav - en - ly peace! birth.

Additional Lyrics

2. Silent night, holy night,
   Shepherds quake at the sight.
   Glories stream from heaven afar,
   Heav'nly hosts sing Alleluia.
   Christ the Savior is born.
   Christ the Savior is born.

3. Silent night, holy night,
   Son of God, love's pure light.
   Radiant beams from Thy holy face,
   With the dawn of redeeming grace.
   Jesus, Lord, at Thy birth.
   Jesus, Lord, at Thy birth.

"The Marvelous Toy"

Tom Paxton wrote this children's song that describes a child's delight in the incomprehensible. Let's use the down-up strum here as well, but this time in 4/4.

Words and Music by
Tom Paxton

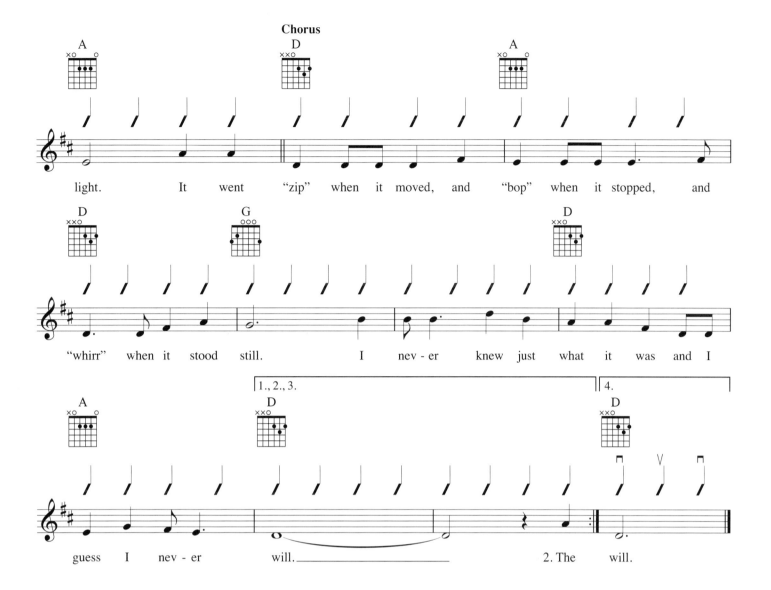

Additional Lyrics

2. The first time that I picked it up, I had a big surprise,
   For right on its bottom were two big buttons that looked like big green eyes.
   I first pushed one and then the other, and then I twisted its lid,
   And when I set it down again, this is what it did: *(To Chorus)*

3. It first marched left and then marched right and then marched under a chair,
   And when l looked where it had gone, it wasn't even there!
   I started to sob and my daddy laughed, for he knew that I would find,
   When l turned around, my marvelous toy, chugging from behind. *(To Chorus)*

4. Well, the years have gone by too quickly, it seems, and I have my own little boy.
   And yesterday I gave to him my marvelous little toy.
   His eyes nearly popped right out of his head, and he gave a squeal of glee.
   Neither one of us knows just what it is, but he loves it, just like me. *(To Chorus)*

"Goin' to the Zoo"

This is another of Tom Paxton's wonderful children's songs. Here, we're going to try something more complicated with the strumming. It's the same down-up strum as in the last song, but this time instead of playing one strum (either down or up) on each beat, you'll play two strums for each quarter note beat (or, more precisely, one strum for each eighth note)—first a downstrum and then an upstrum, like this:

1-and-*2*-and-*3*-and-*4*-and | *1*-and-*2*-and-*3*-and-*4*-and | *etc.*

or

down-up-*down*-up-*down*-up-*down*-up | *down*-up-*down*-up-*down*-up-*down*-up

We'll visit a third Tom Paxton song a little later in the book.

Words and Music by
Tom Paxton

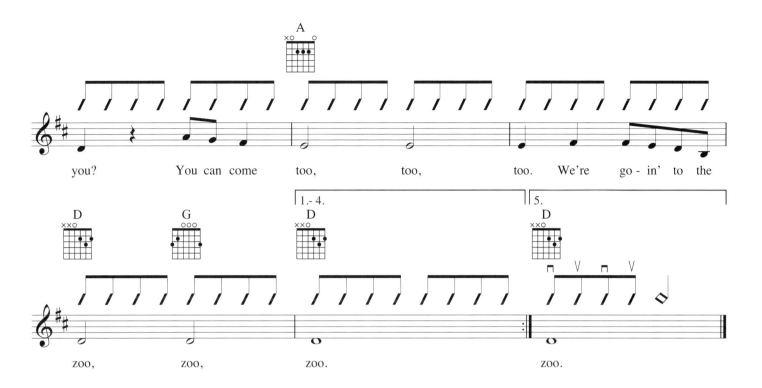

you? You can come too, too, too. We're go-in' to the

zoo, zoo, zoo. zoo.

Additional Lyrics

2. See the elephant with the long trunk swingin',
   Great big ears and the long trunk swingin',
   Sniffin' up the peanuts with the long trunk swingin'.
   We can stay all day. *(To Chorus)*

3. See all the monkeys scritch, scritch, scratchin',
   Jumpin' around and scritch, scritch, scratchin',
   Hangin' by their long tails, skritch, skritch, scratchin'.
   We can stay all day. *(To Chorus)*

4. Seals in the pool, all honk, honk, honkin',
   Catchin' fish and honk, honk, honkin',
   Little seals honk, honk, honkin'.
   We can stay all day. *(To Chorus)*

5. We stayed all day, and we're gettin' sleepy.
   Sittin' in the car and we're sleep, sleep, sleepy.
   Home already and we're sleep, sleep sleepy.
   We have stayed all day. *(To Chorus)*

Alternate Chorus

We've been to the zoo, zoo, zoo.
So have you, you, you.
You came too, too, too.
We've been to the zoo, zoo, zoo.

■ *Two Caribbean Tunes*

The next two songs were made famous by Harry Belafonte way back in 1956. He is still singing them now. Both songs, as well as Belafonte himself, were key elements of the folk song revival of the '50s and '60s. Even though they have been before the public for so long, they nevertheless remain fresh and vivid today.

"Jamaica Farewell"

Although there's a touch of melancholy to this melody, it needs to be played lightly and lyrically.

Words and Music by
Irving Burgie

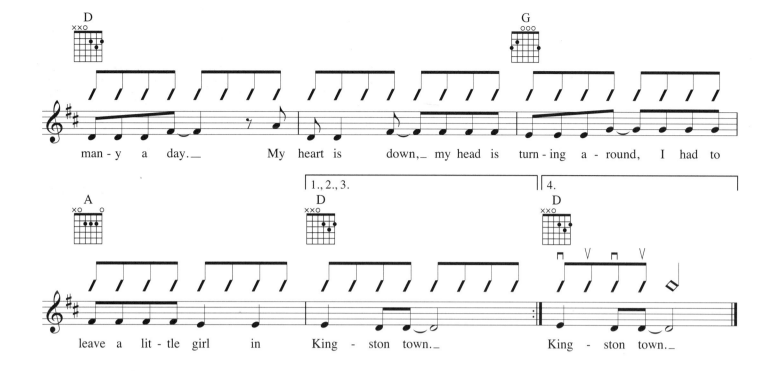

Additional Lyrics

2. Sounds of laughter ev'rywhere
   And the dancing girls swaying to and fro,
   I must declare my heart is there,
   Though I've been from Maine to Mexico. *(To Chorus)*

3. Down at the market you can hear
   Ladies cry out while on their heads they bear
   Ackie, rice; salt fish are nice,
   And the rum is fine any time of year. *(To Chorus)*

4. *Repeat 1st Verse*

"Day-O (The Banana Boat Song)"

Based on a Jamaican folk song, "Day-O" is in some ways an opposite number to "Jamaica Farewell." Although a kind of work song, it is of the more humorous variety. Because of this, it needs to be performed with drama and strength. This works as a counterpoise to the humor.

Do you see that note under the "2" bracket that says "D.S. al Coda"? That stands for "Dal Segno al Coda" in Italian, which means "from the sign to the coda." When you see that, you should jump back to the place where a squiggly mark appears (here, at "Come, Mister tally man") and play until you reach the words "To Coda" and the "o" shape with the cross (here, seven bars after the "segno" squiggle), which means that you now should jump to the Coda of the song. A *Coda*, which in Italian means "tail," is literally that—the tail end of the piece. It is indicated by the word "Coda" and the reappearance of the "o" shape. From there, you simply play to the end.

By the way, that "N.C." near the beginning of the song isn't a new chord! It stands for "No Chord," and it means that you don't play at all until the next chord is indicated.

Words and Music by
Irving Burgie and William Attaway

27

Additional Lyrics

A beautiful bunch a'ripe banana.
Daylight come and me wan' go home.
Hide the deadly black tarant'la.
Daylight come and me wan' go home.
Day, me say day-o.
Daylight come and me wan' go home.
Day, me say day, me say day, me say . . .
Daylight come and me wan' go home.

"The Middle"

Jimmy Eat World—Jim Adkins, Tom Linton, Rick Burch, and Zach Lind—went platinum with their self-titled album in 2002. This number about persistence and being yourself topped the Billboard Modern Rock chart for four weeks.

Words and Music by
James Adkins, Thomas D. Linton,
Richard Burch and Zachary Lind

1. Hey.
2., 3. *See additional lyrics*

Don't write your-self off yet.

It's on-ly in your head you feel left out or looked__ down - on.__

__ Just try your best.__

Try ev-'ry-thing you can. And don't you wor-ry what they

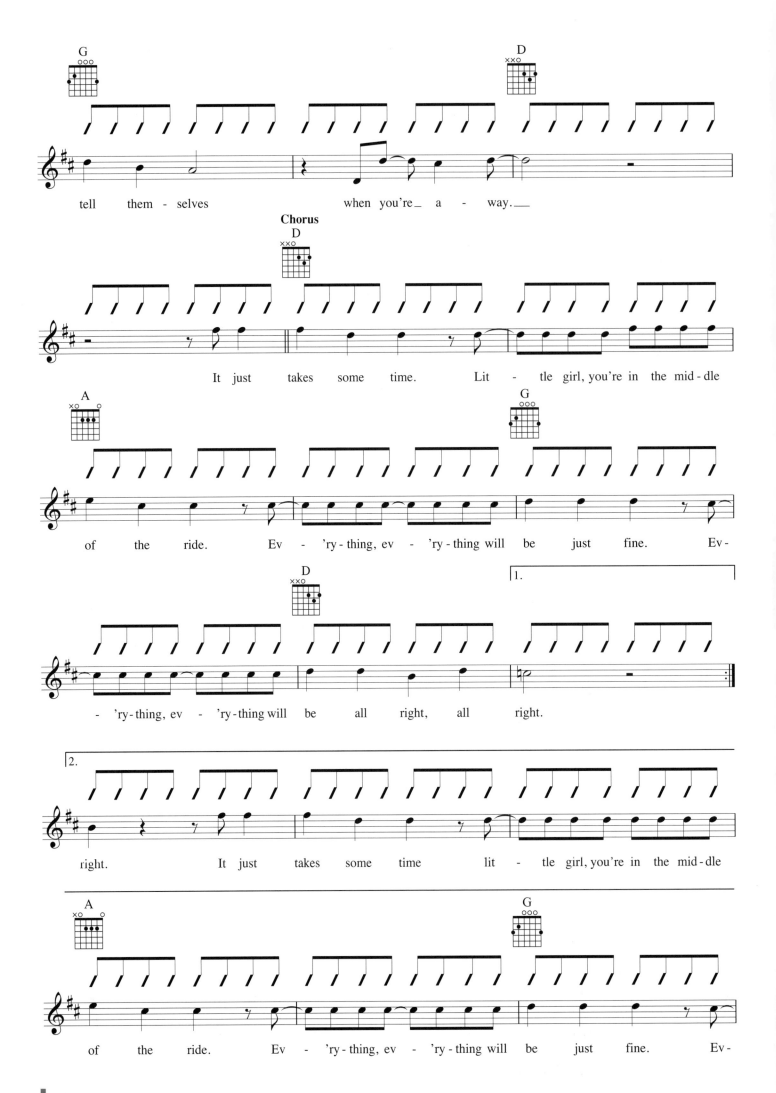

tell them - selves   when you're_ a - way.__

Chorus

It just   takes   some   time.   Lit - tle girl, you're in the mid - dle

of   the   ride.   Ev - 'ry - thing, ev - 'ry - thing will   be   just   fine.   Ev-

1.

- 'ry - thing, ev - 'ry - thing will be   all   right,   all   right.

2.

right.   It just   takes   some   time   lit - tle girl, you're in the mid - dle

of   the   ride.   Ev - 'ry - thing, ev - 'ry - thing will   be   just   fine.   Ev-

D

- 'ry-thing, ev - 'ry-thing will be all right, all right._____

3.

right.   It just takes some time   lit - tle girl, you're in the mid-dle

A   **G**

of the ride.   Ev - 'ry-thing, ev - 'ry-thing will be just fine.   Ev -

D

- 'ry-thing, ev - 'ry-thing will be all right._____

Additional Lyrics

2.   Hey. You know they're all the same.
     You know you're doin' better on your own, so don't give in.
     Live right now. Yeah, just be yourself.
     It doesn't matter if it's good enough for someone else. *(To Chorus)*

3.   Hey. Don't write yourself off yet.
     It's only in your head you feel left out or looked down on.
     Just do your best. Do ev'rything you can.
     And don't you worry what their bitter hearts are gonna say. *(To Chorus)*

"Garden Song"

This song was written by David Mallet. The inspiration for the tune was his own garden in Maine, and the song's simple origins have moved many, many musicians to make it their own. There's a slightly different strumming pattern here to challenge you. You'll do two strums (down-up) on the first beat, then one downstrum each for the second and third beats, and then two strums (down-up) for the fourth beat. You may want to practice this pattern on a D chord and really get the feel of it before you try tackling the song.

Words and Music by
Dave Mallett

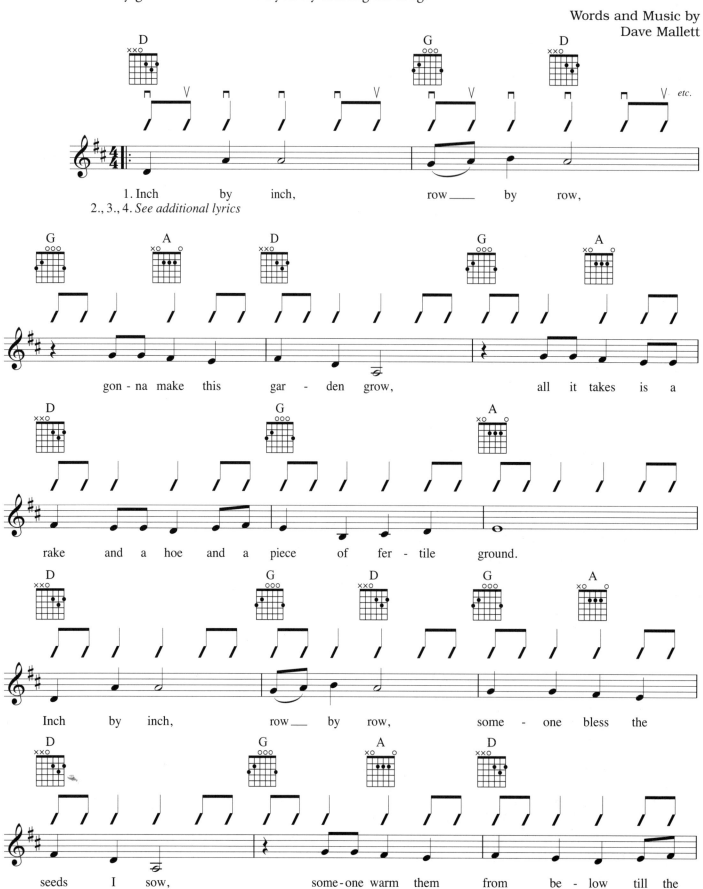

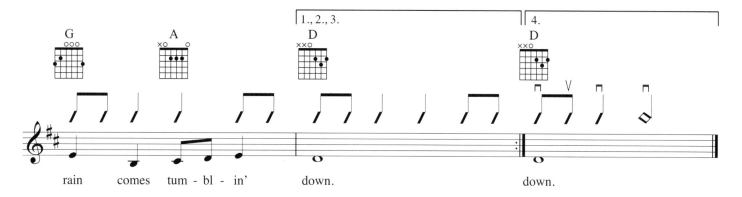

rain   comes   tum - bl - in'   down.   down.

Additional Lyrics

2. Pullin' weeds and pickin' stones,
      We are made of dreams and bones,
      Feel the need to grow my own
      'Cause the time is close at hand.
      Grain for grain, sun and rain
      Find my way in nature's chain,
      Tune my body and my brain
      To the music from the land.

3. Plant your rows straight and long,
      Temper them with prayer and song,
      Mother Earth will make you strong
      If you give her loving care.
      Old crow watching hungrily
      From his perch in yonder tree,
      In my garden I'm as free
      As that feathered thief up there.

4. *Repeat 1st Verse*

■ *Two Songs by Stephen Foster*

There is no one in American musical history who has left such a rich and enduring legacy as Stephen Foster, the composer of our next two songs. His compositions examine romance ("Jeanie with the Light Brown Hair," "Beautiful Dreamer"), nostalgia ("My Old Kentucky Home"), humor ("Oh, Susanna," "Nelly Bly," "Camptown Races"), and plantation life from the Northern perspective ("Old Folks at Home," "Old Black Joe"). Although many of his songs seem dated today, even politically incorrect, his focus in romanticizing American life of the mid-19th century was always one of celebration.

Foster was born on the 4th of July in 1826 in Pittsburgh. An interesting bit of trivia is that this was the same day that both John Adams and Thomas Jefferson died. He wrote his first composition, "Tioga Waltz," at the age of 14. His period of greatest productivity was in the 1850s, when he was living in New York. He died in 1864. Two of his compositions became official state songs: "My Old Kentucky Home" (Kentucky) and "The Old Folks at Home" (Florida).

"Old Folks at Home (Swanee River)"

This was adopted as the official song of the state of Florida in 1935. The accompaniment is reasonably straightforward: a downstrum on 1, another downstrum on 2, a down-up on 3, and then another down-up on 4.

Words and Music by
Stephen C. Foster

2. All 'round the little farm I wandered when I was young,
There many happy days I've squandered, there many the songs I've sung.
When I was playing with my brother, happy was I,
Oh, take me to my kind old mother, there let me live and die. *(To Chorus)*

3. One little hut among the bushes, one that I love,
Still sadly to my memory rushes, no matter where I rove.
When will I see the bees a-humming, all around the comb,
When will I hear the banjo strumming, down in my good old home? *(To Chorus)*

"Oh! Susanna"

This piece is in 2/4, which means that each measure is made up of two quarter notes (which is equal to four eighth notes). And don't let those 16th notes in the strum pattern scare you—they just mean that you play two strums for each eighth note over which they appear.

The key to playing this Stephen Foster song is the lyric, "my banjo on my knee"—the quasi-banjo effect that the accompaniment creates should be light and humorous.

Words and Music by
Stephen C. Foster

Chorus

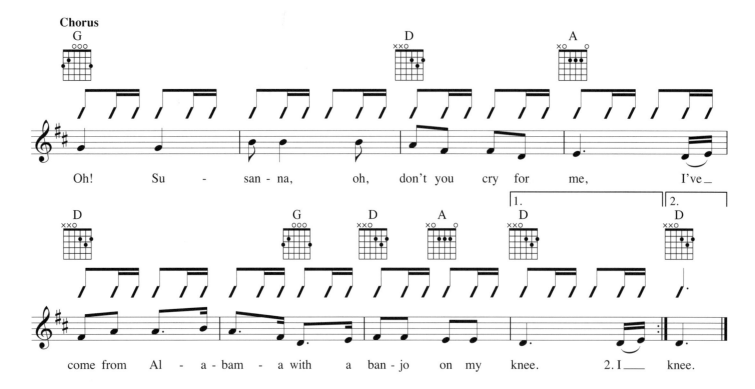

Oh! Su - san - na, oh, don't you cry for me, I've come from Al - a - bam - a with a ban - jo on my knee. 2. I knee.

Additional Lyrics

2. I had a dream the other night,
    When every thing was still.
    I thought I saw Susanna.
    A-comin' down the hill.
    The buckwheat cake was in her mouth,
    The tear was in her eye,
    I said, "I come from Dixie Land.
    Susanna, don't you cry." *(To Chorus)*

"Over the River and Through the Woods"

The words to this song are by Lydia Maria Child; the tune is traditional. The accompaniment is a rollicking affair—give it plenty of bounce. Notice that the song is in 6/8, which means that there are six eighth notes in each measure—think of each measure as two groups of three, with each little group having close to the same "feel" as 3/4. The accompaniment includes a downstrum on the first eighth note, then an upstrum on the third—this pattern is then repeated for the second set of three in the measure, with a downstrum on the fourth eighth note and an upstrum on the sixth (last) eighth note.

Traditional

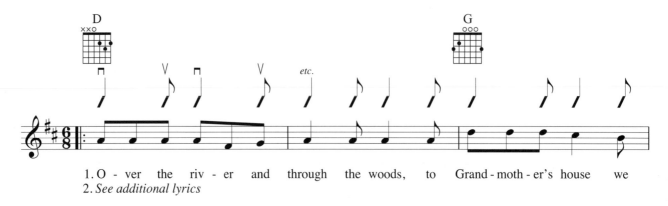

1. O - ver the riv - er and through the woods, to Grand - moth - er's house we
2. *See additional lyrics*

go.＿＿＿ The horse knows the way to car - ry the sleigh through the white and drift - ing snow.＿＿＿ O - ver the riv - er and through the woods, oh how the wind does blow!＿＿＿ It stings the toes and bites the nose as o - ver the ground we go. pie.

Additional Lyrics

2. Over the river and through the woods,
    Trot fast, my dapple gray!
    Spring over the ground like a hunting hound,
    For this is Thanksgiving Day!
    Over the river and through the woods,
    Now Grandmother's cap I spy!
    Hurrah for the fun! Is the pudding done?
    Hurrah for the pumpkin pie!

■ INTRODUCING THE C CHORD

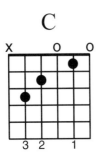

The C chord is formed like the G chord in its bottom two notes, only shifted up one string. When moving from the G chord to the C chord, just shift your second and third fingers over one string together. Then you can, at the same time, release the fourth finger on the top string and put your first finger down at the first fret of the second string. Sound complicated? Work on it a bit until it feels like one smooth motion.

"Auld Lang Syne"

In December of 1788, the Scottish poet Robert Burns included the words for this perennial favorite in a letter to a friend. It was set to a tune that was already very old by Burns' time. Even in Burns' day, there were complaints that the words were sung incorrectly. Since the poetry relies heavily on Scottish dialect, this is not surprising. Today it is indeed difficult to get through the words without a major flub, but the comforting aspect is that probably no one will notice!

By the way, do you see that symbol that looks like a bird's eye over the last note? That's called a *fermata*, and it means that you can hold that last note for as long as you wish.

Words by Robert Burns
Traditional Scottish Melody

Additional Lyrics

2.   And here's a hand, my trusty friend!
     And gie's a hand o' thine!
     We'll take a right gude-willie waught,
     For auld lang syne. *(To Chorus)*

"Leaving on a Jet Plane"

The simple chord progression—just three chords—provides an austere backdrop for complex feelings. This is a John Denver specialty. A simple but forceful strum can provide an appropriate underpinning. This song was also performed by Chantal Kreviazuk for the soundtrack to the movie *Armageddon*.

Words and Music by
John Denver

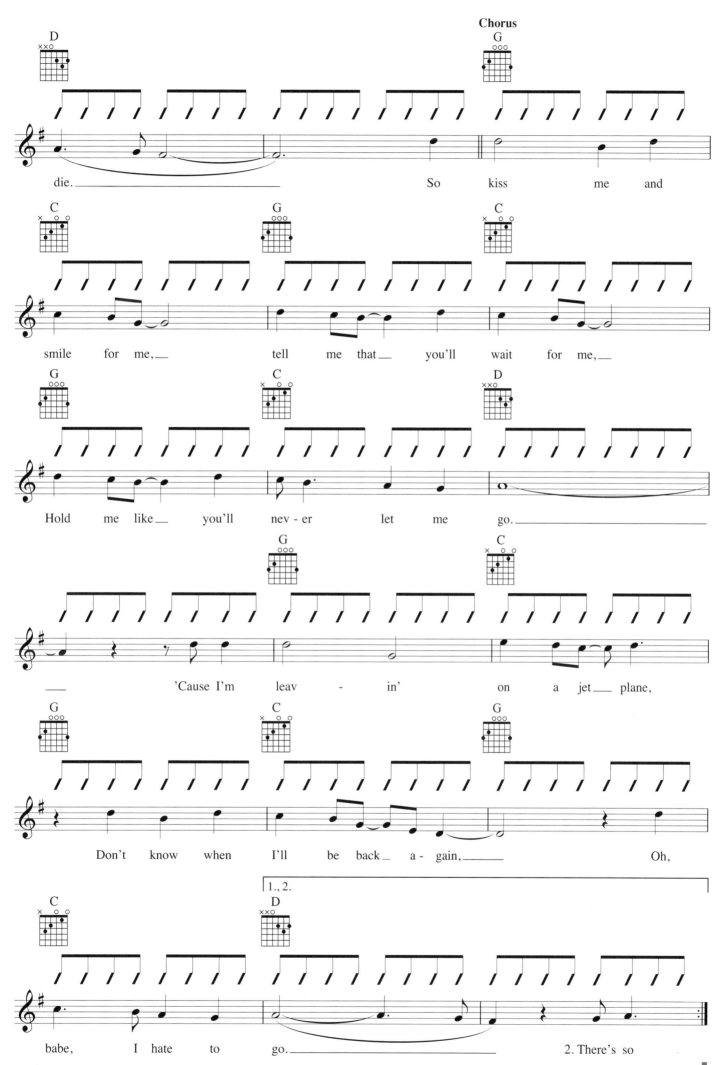

Chorus

die. _____ So kiss me and

smile for me, ___ tell me that ___ you'll wait for me, ___

Hold me like ___ you'll nev - er let me go. _____

___ 'Cause I'm leav - in' on a jet ___ plane,

Don't know when I'll be back ___ a - gain, _____ Oh,

1., 2.

babe, I hate to go. _____ 2. There's so

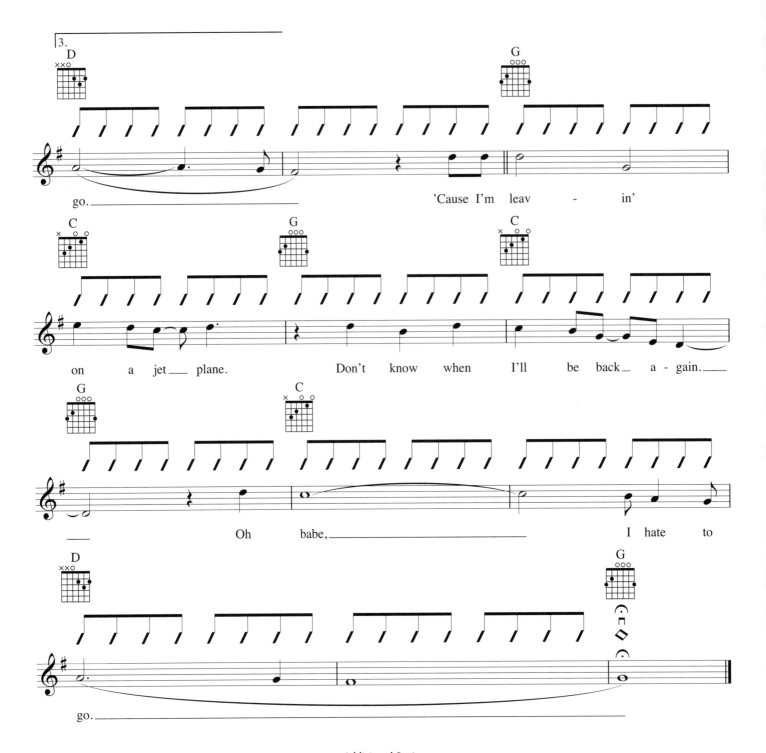

[3.]

D · · · G

go. _____ 'Cause I'm leav - in'

C · G · C

on a jet ___ plane. Don't know when I'll be back ___ a - gain. ___

G · C

___ Oh babe, _____ I hate to

D · G

go. _____

Additional Lyrics

2. There's so many times I've let you down,
    So many times I've played around,
    I tell you now they don't mean a thing.
    Ev'ry place I go, I'll think of you,
    Ev'ry song I sing, I'll sing for you,
    When I come back, I'll wear your wedding ring. *(To Chorus)*

3. Now the time has come to leave you,
    One more time let me kiss you,
    Then close your eyes, I'll be on my way.
    Dream about the days to come
    When I won't have to leave alone,
    About the time I won't have to say: *(To Chorus)*

"The Man on the Flying Trapeze"

We know this song as a light and silly ditty, often accompanying some cartoon. George Leybourne wrote the original version in 1868.

Words by George Leybourne
Music by Alfred Lee

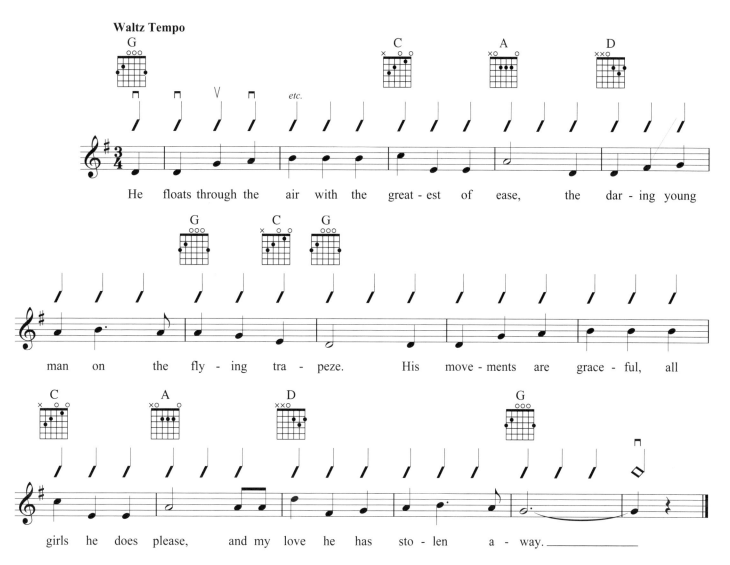

He floats through the air with the great - est of ease, the dar - ing young man on the fly - ing tra - peze. His move - ments are grace - ful, all girls he does please, and my love he has sto - len a - way.

"My Bonnie Lies Over the Ocean"

This is a traditional folk song. Although it was first published in1881, it has certainly been around for a lot longer than that. Try this simple strum on for size, and then make up a new one of your own.

Additional Lyrics

2.   Last night as I lay on my pillow,
     I wondered where Bonnie could be,
     I wished I could sail on the ocean,
     And bring back my Bonnie to me. *(To Chorus)*

"My Dog's Bigger than Your Dog"

Here's another Tom Paxton song. He notes that including children's songs in one's repertoire was part of the tradition of such singers as Pete Seeger, Woody Guthrie, and Jean Ritchie. He himself did an entire album of children's songs. This one has a bit of an adult message along with the kiddy stuff. This two-measure strum pattern can be a little tricky at first, so try it out just on a G chord before you tackle the tune. Notice that the Chorus uses only the second half of the pattern all the way through.

Words and Music by
Tom Paxton

Chorus

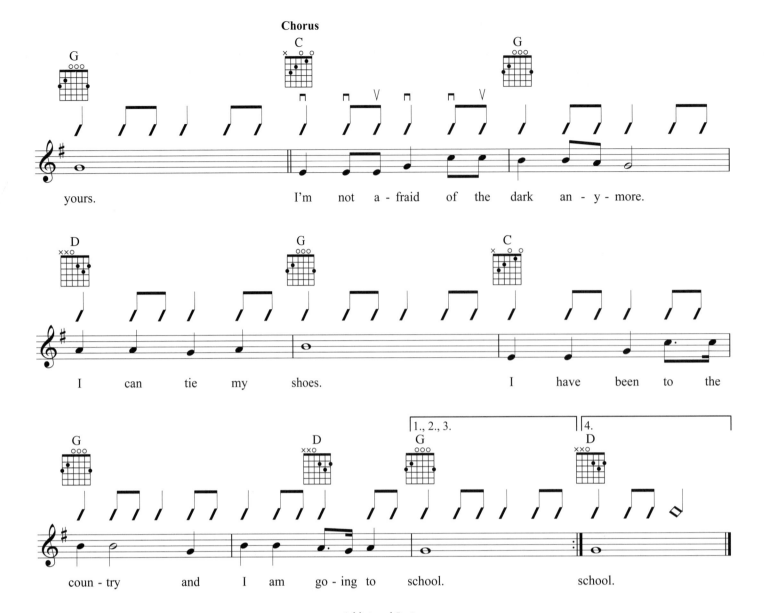

yours.   I'm not a - fraid of the dark an - y - more.

I can tie my shoes.   I have been to the

coun - try and I am go - ing to school.   school.

Additional Lyrics

2. My dad's tougher than your dad.
     My dad's tougher than yours.
     My dad's tougher and he yells louder and
     My dad's tougher than yours.

Answering Verse:
My dad's louder than your dad.
My dad's louder than yours.
Momma buys a new dress, Daddy makes noises.
My dad's louder than yours. *(To Chorus)*

3. Our car's faster than your car.
     Our car's faster than yours.
     It has a louder horn, it bumps other cars.
     Our car's faster than yours.

Answering Verse:
Our car's older than your car.
Our car's older than yours.
It stops running and Daddy kicks the fenders.
Our car's older than yours. *(To Chorus)*

4. My mom's older than your mom.
     My mom's older than yours.
     She takes smelly baths, she hides the gray hairs.
     My mom's older than yours.

Answering Verse:
My mom's funnier than your mom,
My Mom's funnier than yours,
Her hair is pretty and it changes colors,
My Mom's funnier than yours. *(To Chorus)*

"I've Been Working on the Railroad"

Although the origins of this song are unknown, it was probably a work song. With the addition of the Chorus, it has now become a children's classic, both simple and fun to play. The Verse can be done with a real motor feel, chugging away like a steam engine. The Chorus, on the other hand, can be more laid back—let the lyrics sing out while you just back up the voice. Notice that the strum pattern beginning at "Dinah won't you" follows the rhythm of the words.

American Folksong

horn?_____ Di - nah won't you blow, Di - nah won't you blow,

Di - nah won't you blow our horn? Some - one's in the kitch - en with Di - nah,

Some - one's in the kitch - en I know._____ Some - one's in the kitch - en with

Di - nah, Strum - min' on the old ban - jo and sing - in', "Fee - fi -

fid - dl - ee - i - o. Fee - fi - fid - dl - ee - i - o._____ Fee - fi -

fid - dl - ee - i - o." Strum - min' on the old ban - jo.

INTRODUCING THE E MINOR CHORD

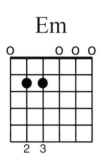

Em

The E minor chord is the easiest of all chords to play; it is also the most "open," since it uses only two stopped notes and it sounds best with all the strings ringing. This means that you can easily boom out with it, so be careful not to outbalance the other chords in a song.

"Swing Low, Sweet Chariot"

This traditional spiritual should be played with a smooth, connected strum on the Chorus. For the Verses, you might want to wail a bit.

Do you see that "Fine" at the end of the Chorus? That means "end," and what it signifies is that after you've sung the last Verse and have returned back to the Chorus, the song ends there.

Traditional Spiritual

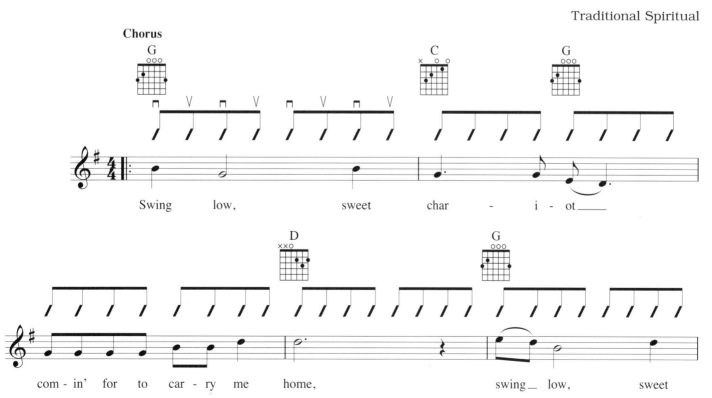

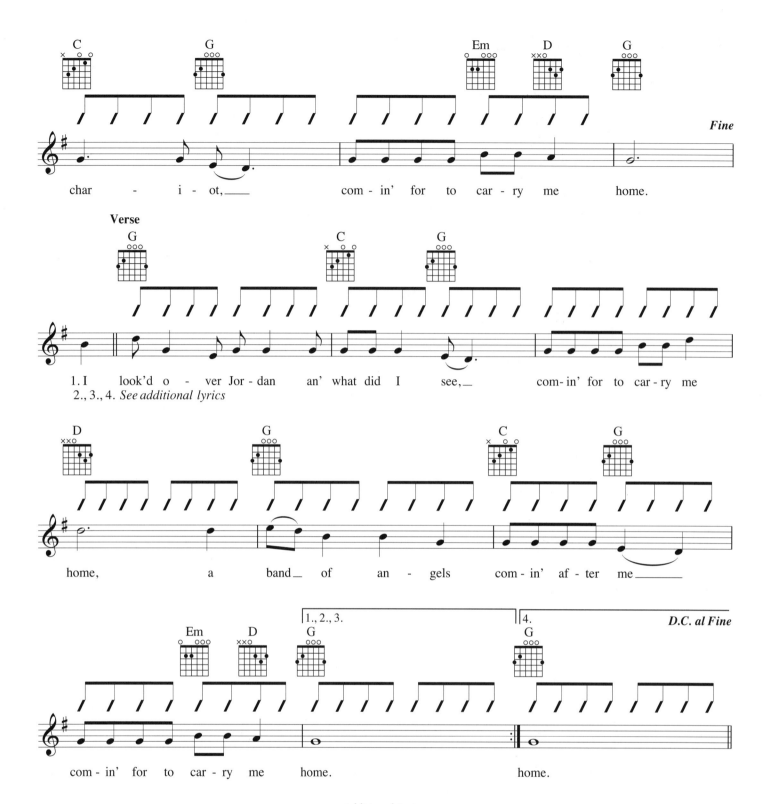

Additional Lyrics

2. If you get to heaven before I do,
   Comin' for to carry me home,
   Tell all my friends I'm comin' there too,
   Comin' for to carry me home. *(To Chorus)*

3. I'm sometimes up and sometimes down,
   Comin' for to carry me home,
   But still my soul feels heaven bound,
   Comin' for to carry me home. *(To Chorus)*

4. If I get there before you do,
   Comin' for to carry me home,
   I'll cut a hole and pull you through,
   Comin' for to carry me home. *(To Chorus)*

■ *Two Songs by John Denver*

From a background as the son of an Air Force officer, Henry John Deutschendorf, Jr., moved around a lot in his youth. When he moved to Los Angeles to pursue a career in music, he changed his name to John Denver, which helped to maintain his connection to Colorado, the state of his birth. After his selection as the lead singer of the Mitchell Trio, then the great success of his song "Leaving on a Jet Plane" (which was recorded by the group Peter, Paul and Mary), he emerged into a culture that was ready to embrace his clarity, simplicity, and homespun social sentiment. With the creation of a substantial body of compositions, including songs like "Take Me Home, Country Roads," "Rocky Mountain High," "Sunshine on My Shoulders," "Annie's Song," "Back Home Again," "Thank God I'm a Country Boy," and "Calypso," he was on his way to becoming a cultural icon as a singer-songwriter. His focus on environmental preservation reflected his roots in the folk music revival. However, no one else from that era went on to achieve such success in the world of commercial music. This enabled him to bring his message to a wide international audience.

Here are two songs for now—you'll encounter even more John Denver songs a little later in the book.

"Take Me Home, Country Roads"

John Denver co-wrote this hit with his two close friends, Bill and Taffy Danoff. Its success following its release in May of 1971 cemented a friendship that lasted many years. This song is a kind of anthem for the University of West Virginia.

Words and Music by
John Denver, Bill Danoff and Taffy Nivert

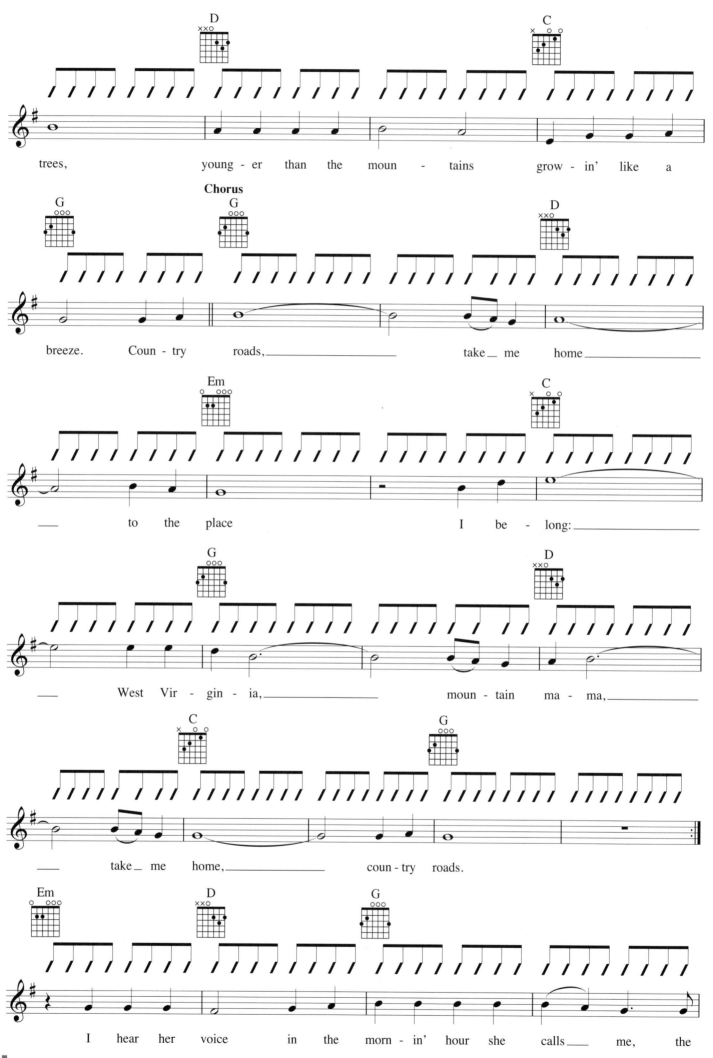

trees, young - er than the moun - tains grow - in' like a

Chorus

breeze. Coun - try roads,_____ take __ me home _____

____ to the place I be - long:_____

____ West Vir - gin - ia,_____ moun - tain ma - ma,_____

____ take __ me home,_____ coun - try roads.

I hear her voice in the morn - in' hour she calls ___ me, the

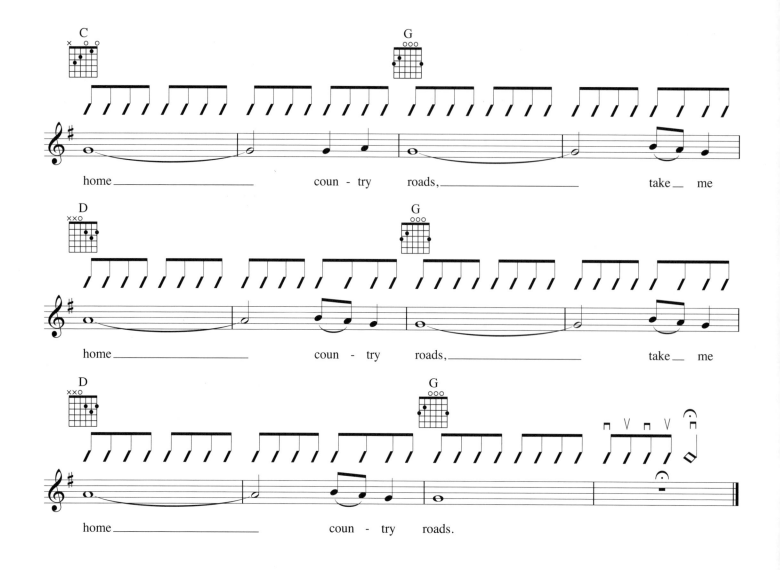

home _____ coun - try roads, _____ take __ me

home _____ coun - try roads, _____ take __ me

home _____ coun - try roads.

Additional Lyrics

2.   All my memories gather round her,
     Miner's lady, stranger to blue water.
     Dark and dusty, painted on the sky,
     Misty taste of moonshine, teardrop in my eye.

"Rocky Mountain High"

This is John Denver's "theme song," if he had one. It is about, among other things, his home state of Colorado, and all that meant to him. What it means to us includes such things as the transforming power of our natural resources, including the Rocky Mountains; the meditative experience of solitude; the breath-taking beauty of nature, when we take the time to let it in; and many other things, special to each of us. The accompaniment here is quite regular, but don't let it get burdensome.

Words and Music by
John Denver and Mike Taylor

Moderately slow

1. He was born____ in the sum - mer of his twen-ty - sev-enth year____

2.-5. *See additional lyrics*

____ com - in' home to a place he'd nev - er been_ be - fore._

He left yes - ter - day _ be - hind___ him,____ you might

say he was born_ a - gain.___ You might say he found the key _ for ev - 'ry door._

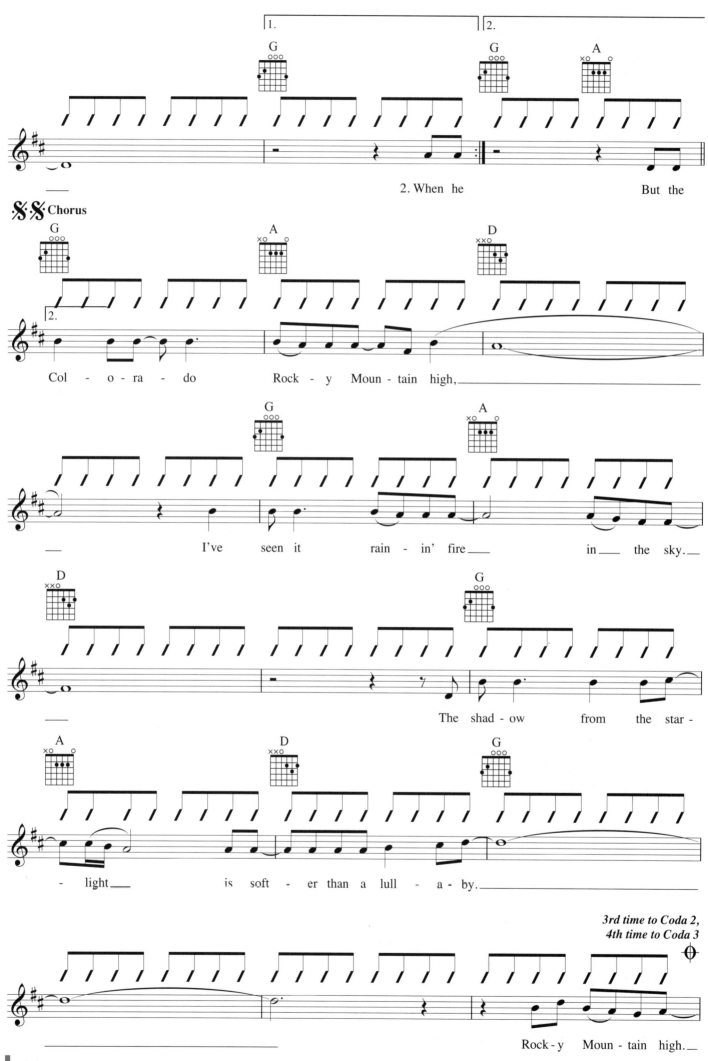

2. When he   But the

S.S. Chorus

Col - o - ra - do   Rock - y   Moun - tain high,

I've   seen it   rain - in' fire   in   the sky.

The shad - ow   from   the star -

- light   is soft - er than a lull - a - by.

3rd time to Coda 2,
4th time to Coda 3

Rock - y   Moun - tain high.

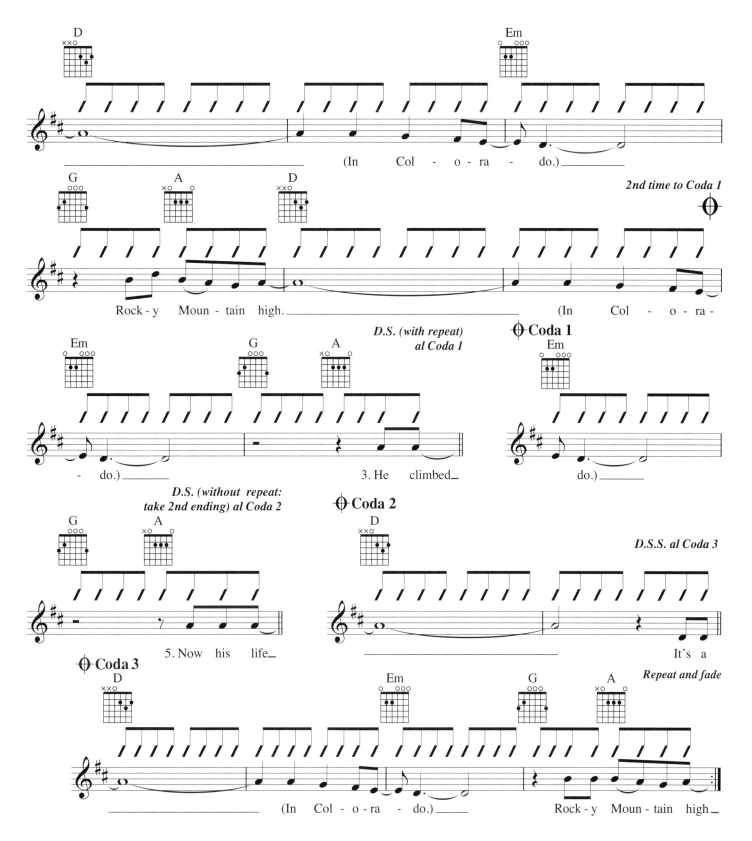

Additional Lyrics

2. When he first came to the mountains his life was far away,
    On the road and hangin' by a song.
    But the string's already broken and he doesn't really care.
    It keeps changin' fast, and it don't last for long. *(To Chorus 1)*

3. He climbed cathedral mountains, he saw silver clouds below,
    He saw everything as far as you can see.
    And they say that he got crazy once and he tried to touch the sun,
    And he lost a friend but kept his memory.

4. Now he walks in quiet solitude the forests and the streams
    Seeking grace in every step he takes.
    His sight has turned inside himself to try and understand
    The serenity of a clear blue mountain lake. *(To Chorus 2)*

57

Chorus 2:
And The Colorado Rocky Mountain high
I've seen it rainin' fire in the sky.
You can talk to God and listen to the casual reply.
Rocky Mountain high. (In Colorado.)
Rocky Mountain high. (In Colorado.)

5. Now his life if full of wonder, but his heart still knows some fear
    Of a simple thing he cannot comprehend.
    Why they try to tear the mountains down to bring in a couple more,
    More people, more scars upon the land. *(To Chorus 3)*

Chorus 3:
And the Colorado Rocky Mountain high,
I've seen it rainin' fire in the sky.
I know he'd be a poorer man if he never saw an eagle fly.
Rocky Mountain high.

Chorus 4:
It's a Colorado Rocky Mountain high,
I've seen it rainin' fire in the sky.
Friends around the campfire and everybody's high.
Rocky Mountain high. (In Colorado.)

"Time Is on My Side"

This is the classic Stones hit from the '60s. Don't let that 12/8 time signature scare you: it's just four sets of three eighth notes. Think of it as a sort of "4/4," but with each beat actually made up of three smaller beats. You strum on the first and last part of each of these beats.

Words and Music by
Jerry Ragovoy

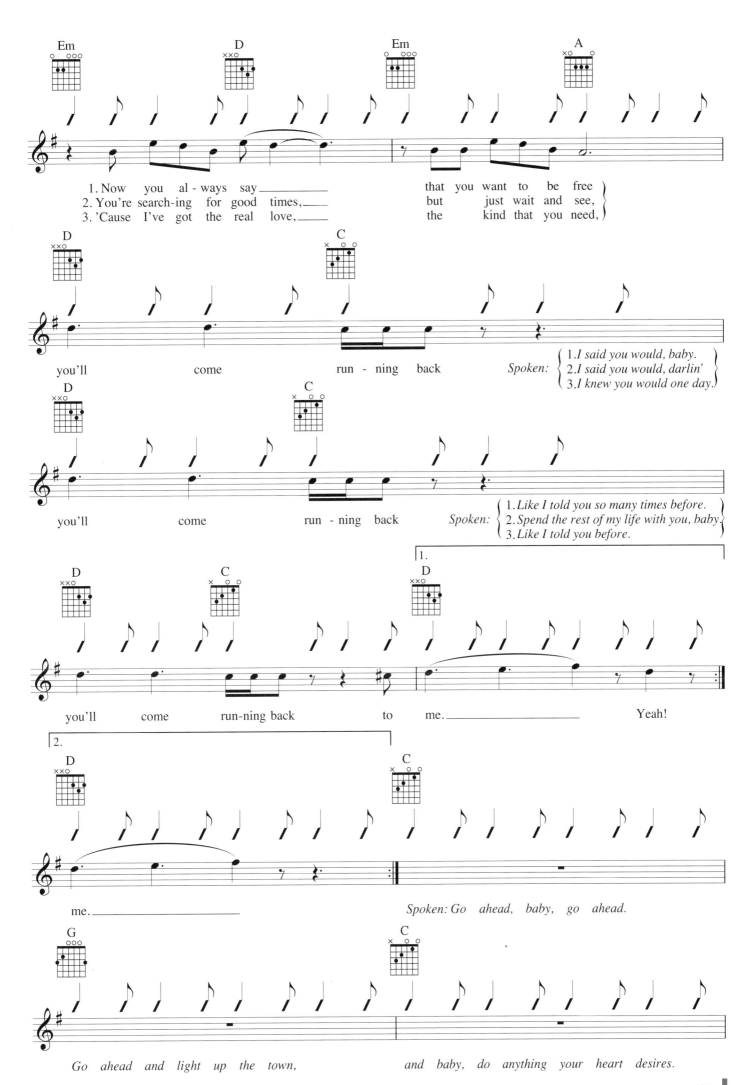

1. Now you al - ways say ____ that you want to be free
2. You're search-ing for good times, ____ but just wait and see,
3. 'Cause I've got the real love, ____ the kind that you need,

you'll come run - ning back   Spoken: { 1. I said you would, baby.
                                          2. I said you would, darlin'
                                          3. I knew you would one day. }

you'll come run - ning back   Spoken: { 1. Like I told you so many times before.
                                          2. Spend the rest of my life with you, baby.
                                          3. Like I told you before. }

1.
you'll come run-ning back   to   me. ____ Yeah!

2.
me. ____

Spoken: Go ahead, baby, go ahead.

Go ahead and light up the town,   and baby, do anything your heart desires.

Remember, I'll always be 'round, and I know, I know like I told you so many times before,

You're gonna come back. Yeah you're gonna come back, baby, knockin', yeah, knockin'. Yeah, knockin'

D.C. al Coda   Coda

on my door, yeah.   me._____

Time,   time,   time   is on my___ side._____ (Yes, it is.)_____

Time,   time,   time   is on my___ side._____ (Yes, it is.)_____

Time,   time,   time   is on my___ side._____

"Puff the Magic Dragon"

Lenny Lipton was a college student at Cornell in Ithaca, New York. One day while visiting his friend, he sat down at the friend's roommate's typewriter. Feeling somewhat saddened by the weight of adult responsibilities, he wrote a short poem about a carefree child's imaginings. Feeling a bit better after banging out the poem, he left. The roommate, Peter Yarrow, returned later and saw the poem in his typewriter. He liked it, and added a melody to it and actually began singing it around Ithaca. Later on, he became a member of a group (Peter, Paul and Mary), and they liked it and sang it with him. Eventually (in 1963) the song became a big hit. In the kind of story ending one seldom hears, Peter tracked down Lenny and made sure that he received his share of the royalties.

Words and Music by
Lenny Lipton and Peter Yarrow

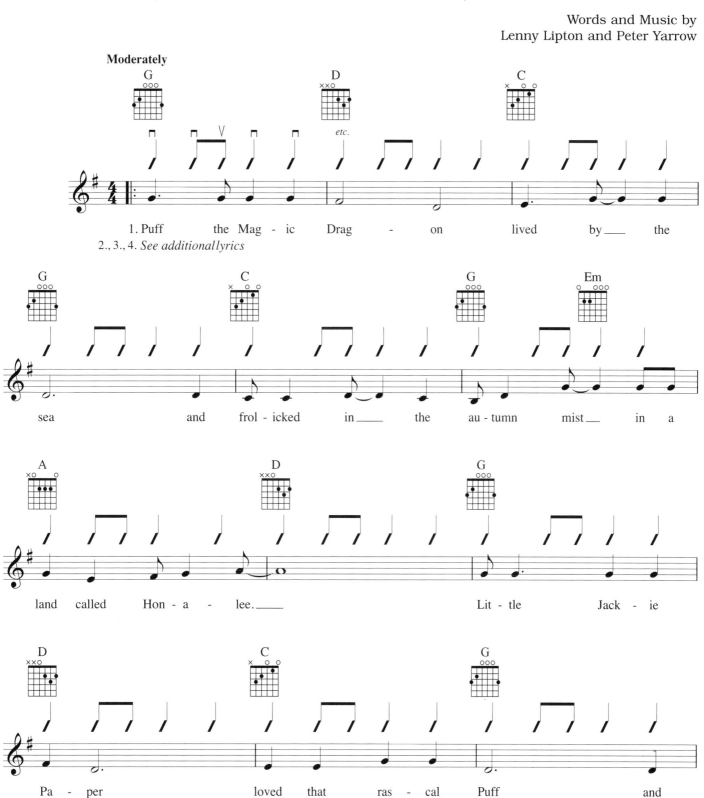

Chorus

brought   him   strings   and   seal - ing   wax ____   and   oth - er   fan - cy

stuff.   Oh!   Puff   the   Mag - ic   Drag - - - on

lived   by ____   the   sea   and   frol - icked   in ____   the

au - tumn   mist ____   in   a   land   called   Hon - a - lee. ____

Puff   the   Mag - ic   Drag - - - on   lived   by ____   the

sea   and   frol - icked   in ____   the   au - tumn   mist ____   in   a

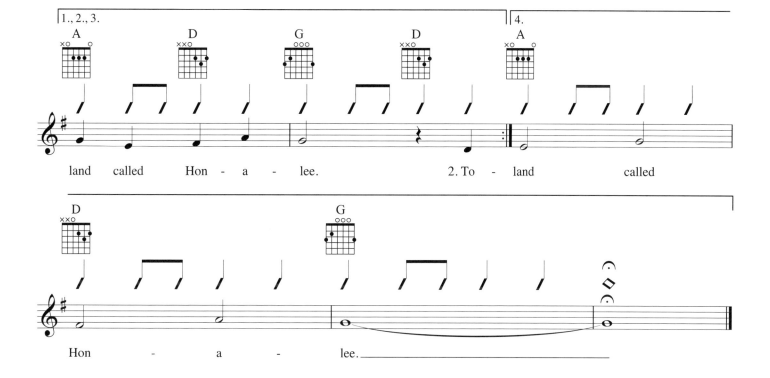

land   called   Hon - a - lee.   2. To - land   called

Hon - a - lee.

Additional Lyrics

2.   Together they would travel on a boat with billowed sail.
     Jackie kept a lookout perched on Puff's gigantic tail.
     Noble kings and princes would bow whene'er they came.
     Pirate ships would low'r their flags when Puff roared out his name. Oh!

3.   A dragon lives forever, but not so little boys.
     Painted wings and giant rings make way for other toys.
     One gray night it happened, Jackie Paper came no more,
     And Puff that mighty dragon, he ceased his fearless roar. Oh!

4.   His head was bent in sorrow, green tears fell like rain.
     Puff no longer wanted to play along the Cherry Lane.
     Without his lifelong friend, Puff could not be brave,
     So Puff that mighty dragon sadly slipped into his cave. Oh!

INTRODUCING THE A MINOR CHORD

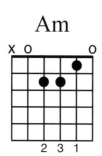

Am

"Home on the Range"

The music to this, the official song of the state of Kansas, was originally written out on a piece of brown wrapping paper in 1873, albeit Dr. Brewster M. Higley wrote the lyrics (as a poem) a couple of years before that. On Higley's arrival in Gaylord, Kansas, he showed it to a former Union Army bugler named Dan Kelly. Kelly must have been quite taken with it, since he wrote a melody setting the words of the poem, working it out on the violin. He then played it the next night when he went calling on a lady friend, Miss Lulu. That worked out so well, he played it at a dance the next Friday night. After the dance, the song spread like wildfire through the country, and the rest was history.

Lyrics by Dr. Brewster Higley
Music by Dan Kelly

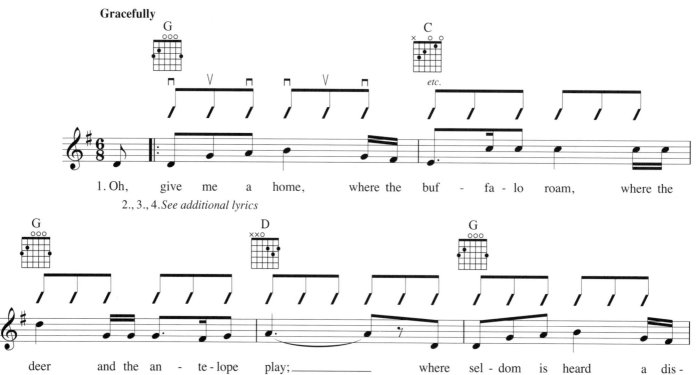

Chorus

cour - ag - ing word, and the skies are not cloud - y all day.____

Home, home on the range,____ where the deer and the an - te - lope

play;____ where sel - dom is heard a dis - cour - ag - ing word, and the

1., 2., 3.   *4.*

skies are not cloud - y all day.____ 2. How day.____

Additional Lyrics

2.   How often at night when the heavens are bright
   With the light of the glittering stars;
   Have I stood there amazed and asked as I gazed
   If their glory exceeds that of ours. *(To Chorus)*

3.   I love the wild flowers in this dear land of ours,
   The curlew I love to hear scream,
   I love the white rocks and the antelope flocks,
   That graze on the mountain so green. *(To Chorus)*

4.   Where the air is so clear and the zephyrs so free,
   The breezes so balmy and light,
   I would not exchange my home on the range
   For all of the cities so bright. *(To Chorus)*

"My Country, 'Tis of Thee (America)"

This is really our second national anthem. The original melody is "God Save the King," the English national anthem. The Rev. Samuel F. Smith penned the words used for our version. A full and stately strum is needed here, of course.

Words by Samuel Francis Smith
Music from Thesaurus Musicus

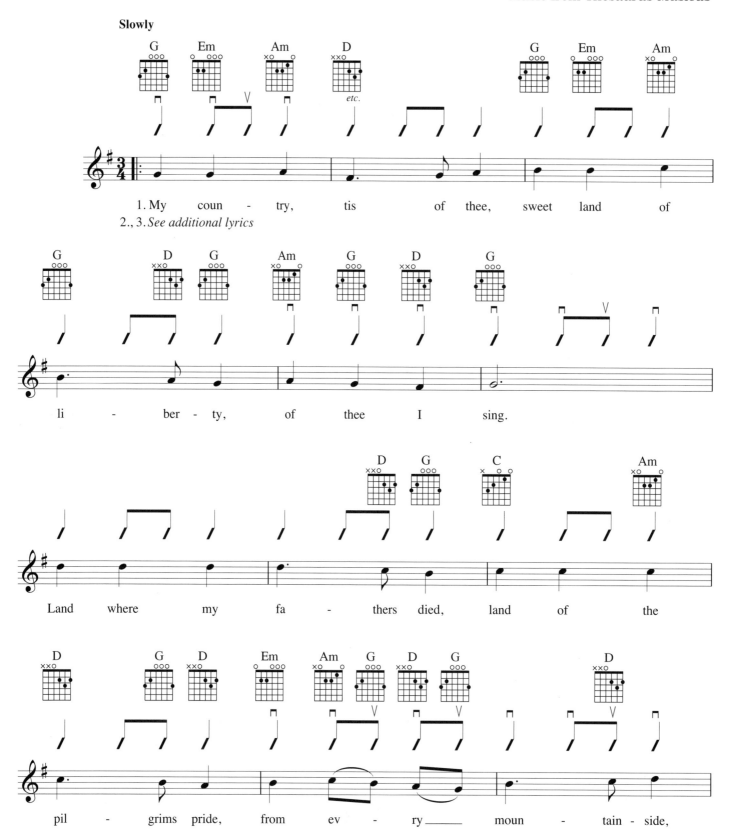

lyrics:

1. My coun - try, tis of thee, sweet land of
2., 3. *See additional lyrics*

li - ber - ty, of thee I sing.

Land where my fa - thers died, land of the

pil - grims pride, from ev - ry____ moun - tain - side,

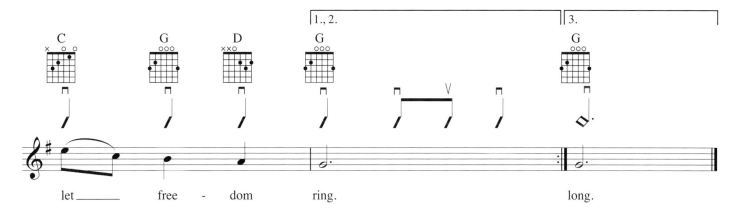

let _____ free - dom ring. long.

Additional Lyrics

2. My native country, thee,
   Land of the noble free,
   Thy name I love;
   I love thy rocks and rills,
   Thy woods and templed hills,
   My heart with rapture thrills
   Like that above.

3. Let music swell the breeze,
   And ring from all the trees
   Sweet Freedom's song;
   Let mortal tongues awake;
   Let all that breathe partake;
   Let rocks their silence break,
   The sound prolong.

"From a Distance"

Julie Gold wrote this song in 1985, just before her 30th birthday. For her, it was the expression of the accumulation of the experiences she had growing up in the '60s.

Words and Music by
Julie Gold

1. From a dis - tance, the world looks blue and green, and the
2., 3. *See additional lyrics*

snow - capped moun - tains white ____ From a dis - tance, the o - cean meets ____

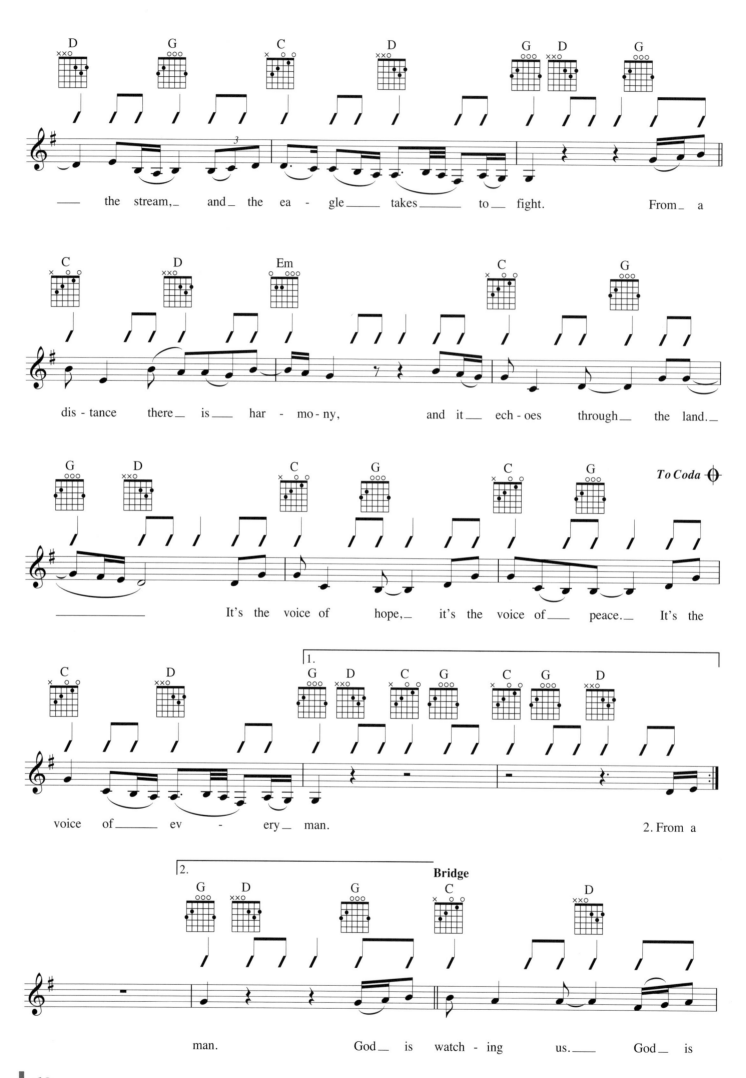

the stream,___ and_ the ea - gle____ takes____ to_ fight. From_ a

dis - tance there_ is___ har - mo - ny, and it ___ ech - oes through___ the land._

_____ It's the voice of hope,___ it's the voice of____ peace.___ It's the

1.

voice of _____ ev - ery_ man.

2. From a

2.

Bridge

man.

God_ is watch - ing us.___ God_ is

watch - ing   us.____   God_ is watch - ing us   from a   dis - tance.___

D.S. al Coda

3. From a

Coda

heart_____ of ev   -   ery__ man._____   It's the

hope of __ hopes,   it's the love of __ loves.__   This is the   song__ of ____ ev   -   ery

Bridge

man._____   And God__ is   watch - ing   us.___   God__ is

69

watch - ing us _____ God _____ is watch - ing us from a _____

dis - tance. _____ Oh, God is _____ watch - ing us _____ from a

dis - tance.

Additional Lyrics

2. From a distance, we all have enough,
    And no one is in need.
    There are no guns, no bombs, no diseases,
    No hungry mouths to feed.
    From a distance, we are instruments
    Marching in a common band;
    Playing songs of hope, playing songs of peace,
    They're the songs of every man. *(To Bridge)*

3. From a distance, you look like my friend
    Even though we are at war.
    From a distance I just cannot comprehend
    What all this fighting is for.
    From a distance there is harmony
    And it echoes through the land.
    It's the hope of hopes, it's the love of loves.
    It's the heart of every man. *(To Coda)*

■ *A Couple of Christmas Carols*

"The Twelve Days of Christmas"

The 12 days referred to here are those of the traditional Christmas season, beginning on Christmas itself and ending on the Feast of the Epiphany. There have been many speculations on the meanings of the 12 presents assigned to each of the days. Probably our best hope for understanding the meanings is simply to enjoy the music and the playful spirit of the lyrics.

An especially satisfying way of playing this song, if there are enough people around, is to assign each of the presents to a different person, who then must come in at the appropriate time in each Verse. But whether it's done with many or with one, the accompaniment must always follow the singing, which can vary in tempo quite a bit.

Traditional English Carol

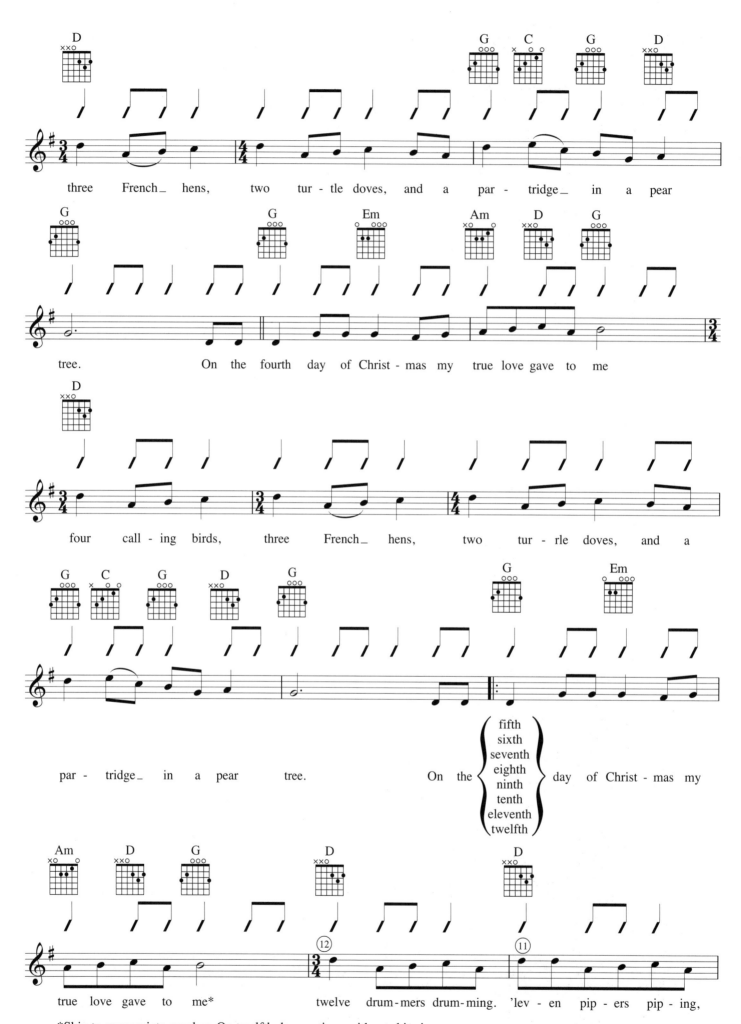

three French_ hens, two tur-tle doves, and a par-tridge_ in a pear tree.

On the fourth day of Christ-mas my true love gave to me

four call-ing birds, three French_ hens, two tur-rle doves, and a

par-tridge_ in a pear tree.

On the { fifth sixth seventh eighth ninth tenth eleventh twelfth } day of Christ-mas my

true love gave to me*

twelve drum-mers drum-ming. 'lev-en pip-ers pip-ing,

*Skip to appropriate number. On twelfth day continue without skipping.

"O Christmas Tree"

This popular Christmas carol, which originally had German lyrics ("O Tannenbaum") shares its tune with the official state song of Maryland—"Maryland, My Maryland."

Traditional German Carol

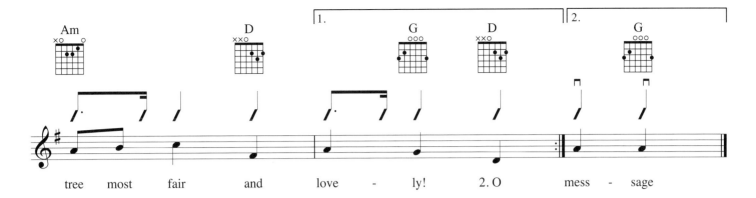

tree most fair and love - ly! 2. O mess - sage

Additional Lyrics

2. O Christmas tree, o Christmas tree!
Thou hast a wondrous message.
O Christmas tree, o Christmas tree!
Thou hast a wondrous message.
Thou dost proclaim the Savior's birth,
Good will to men and peace on Earth.
O Christmas tree, o Christmas tree!
Thou hast a wondrous message.

■ *Percussive Sounds*

There are lots of sounds you can make with an acoustic guitar in addition to plucking and strumming the strings. Slapping the sides, playing completely muffled chords, plucking strings at the end of the neck just past the nut, and many other percussive elements have been used to add more colors to the guitarist's palette. Flamenco players have been using a *golpe* (slap on the bridge) for hundreds of years. Here's how to make that sound: Hold down a chord with the left hand. Slap the *bridge* (the part on the body of the guitar—not the neck—where the strings are anchored) smartly with your right; the chord will ring out after the smacking sound. Note that below, "slap" indicates a *golpe* on the bridge.

"Bingo"

Traditional

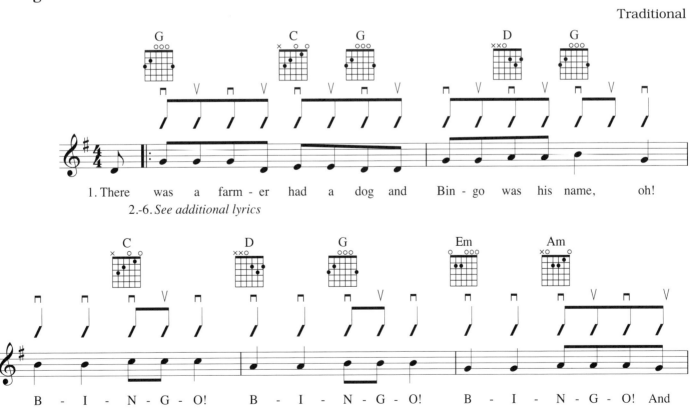

1. There was a farm - er had a dog and Bin - go was his name, oh!
2.-6. *See additional lyrics*

B - I - N - G - O! B - I - N - G - O! B - I - N - G - O! And

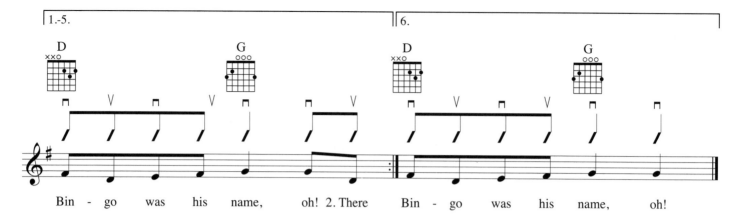

Bin - go was his name, oh! 2. There   Bin - go was his name, oh!

Additional Lyrics

2. There was a farmer had a dog
    and Bingo was his name, oh!
    (Slap)-I-N-G-O!
    (Slap)-I-N-G-O!
    (Slap)-I-N-G-O!
    And Bingo was his name, oh!

3. There was a farmer had a dog
    and Bingo was his name, oh!
    (Slap, slap)-N-G-O!
    (Slap, slap)-N-G-O!
    (Slap, slap)-N-G-O!
    And Bingo was his name, oh!

4. There was a farmer had a dog
    and Bingo was his name, oh!
    (Slap, slap, slap)-G-O!
    (Slap, slap, slap)-G-O!
    (Slap, slap, slap)-G-O!
    And Bingo was his name, oh!

5. There was a farmer had a dog
    and Bingo was his name, oh!
    (Slap, slap, slap, slap)-O!
    (Slap, slap, slap, slap)-O!
    (Slap, slap, slap, slap)-O!
    And Bingo was his name, oh!

6. There was a farmer had a dog and Bingo was his name, oh!
    (Slap, slap, slap, slap, slap)
    (Slap, slap, slap, slap, slap)
    (Slap, slap, slap, slap, slap)
    And Bingo was his name, oh!

■ *More Songs by John Denver*

"I'm Sorry"

John Denver wrote this for his album *Windsong*.

Words and Music by
John Denver

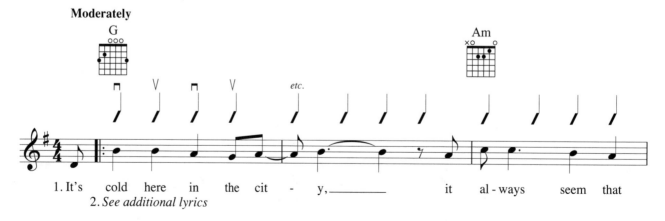

1. It's cold here in the cit - y, _____ it al - ways seem that
2. *See additional lyrics*

Additional Lyrics

2. Our friends all ask about you, I say you're doin' fine
    I expect to hear from you almost anytime.
    But they all know I'm cryin', that I can't sleep at night,
    They all know I'm dyin' down deep inside. *(To Chorus 2)*

Chorus 2:
I'm sorry for all the lies I told you,
I'm sorry for the things I didn't say,
But more than anything else, I'm sorry for myself
I can't believe you went away.

Chorus 3:
I'm sorry if I took some things for granted,
I'm sorry for the chains I put on you,
But more than anything else I'm sorry for myself
For living without you.

"Fly Away"

This 1975 duet was a hit for Olivia Newton-John and John Denver. Olivia recorded many of John Denver's songs in the '70s.

Words and Music by
John Denver

Life in a high - rise can   make   you hun - gry   for
She lis - tens for laugh - ter and   sounds   of danc - ing,   she

things that you   can't__ e - ven see.__   Fly a - way,_____

fly a - way,_____   fly a - way__

In this whole world__ there's no - bod - y as lone - ly as she._____   there's

no - where to go__ and there's no - where that she'd__ rath - er be.__

Coda
G

2.
D. C. al Coda

1.

She's

80

"Annie's Song"

John Denver wrote this song for his wife Annie while skiing in Colorado after a particularly rocky time in their relationship.

Words and Music by
John Denver

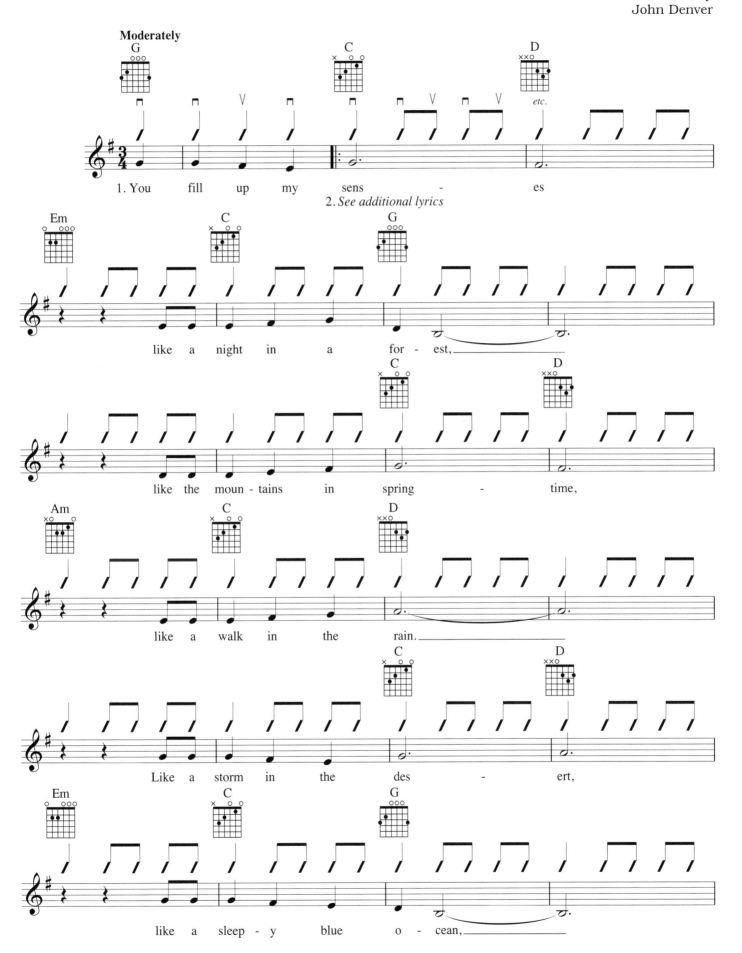

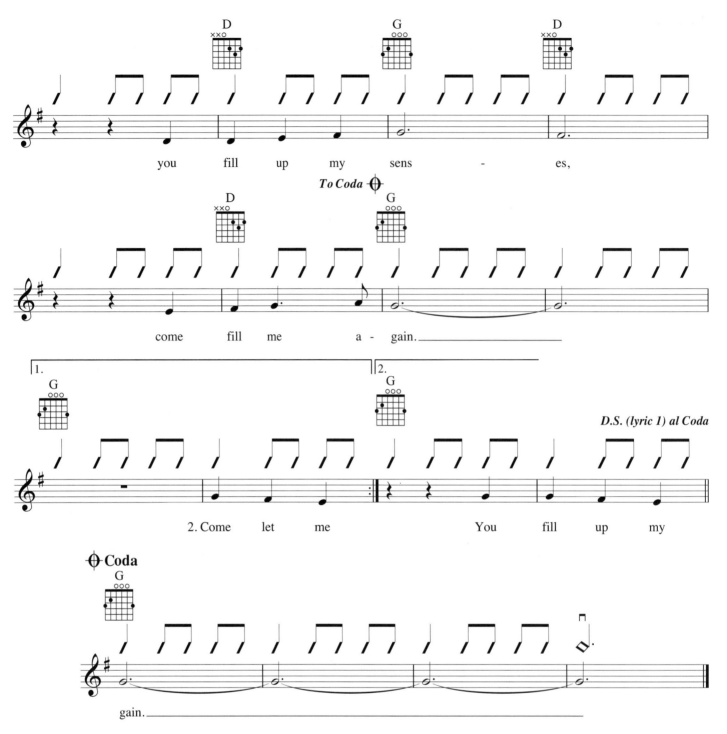

To Coda ⊕

you fill up my sens - es,

come fill me a - gain. _____

1. | **2.**

D.S. (lyric 1) al Coda

2. Come let me   You fill up my

⊕ **Coda**

gain. _____

Additional Lyrics

2.   Come let me love you, let me give my life to you,
Let me drown in your laughter, let me die in your arms,
Let me lay down beside you, let me always be with you,
Come let me love you, come love me again.

"Follow Me"

This next heartfelt song by Denver made its way into more than a few wedding ceremonies in the 1970s.

Words and Music by
John Denver

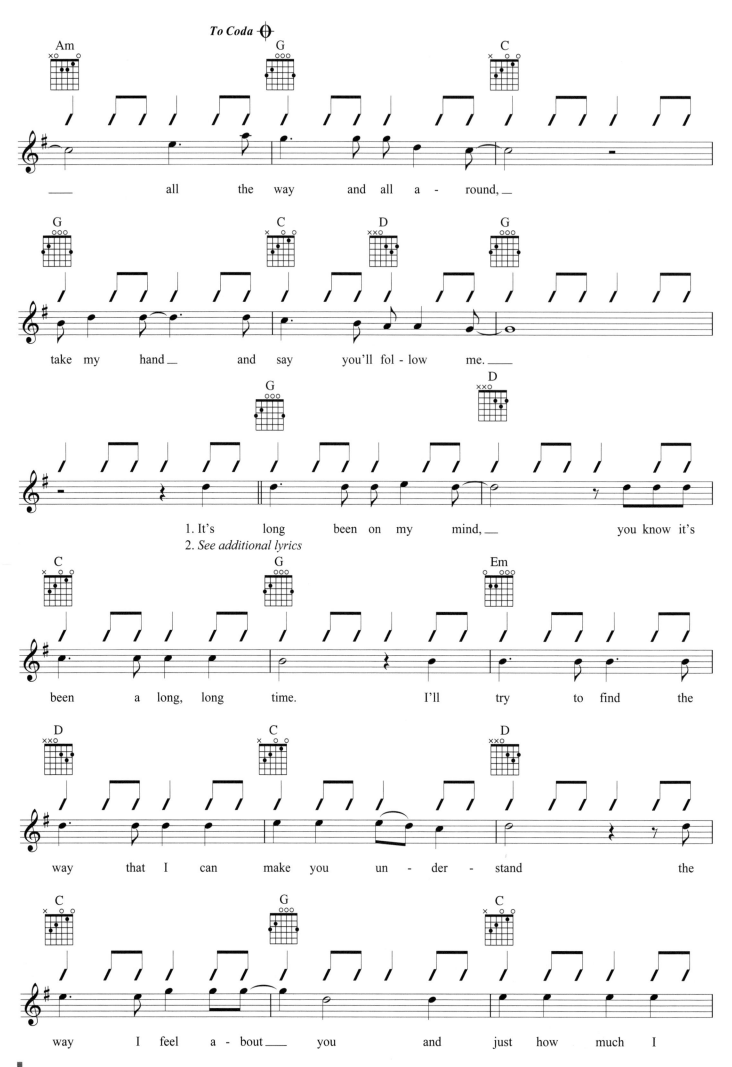

Additional Lyrics

2. You see, I'd like to share my life with you and show you things I've seen,
Places that I'm going to, places where I've been,
To have you there beside me and never be alone.
All the time that you're with me, then we will be at home. *(To Chorus)*

"Back Home Again"

The imagery of this ballad is all-American—rough-hewn in a modern version of a Western love song. The accompaniment has to have a relaxed feel, with the upstrokes lightly accenting the downstrokes.

Words and Music by
John Denver

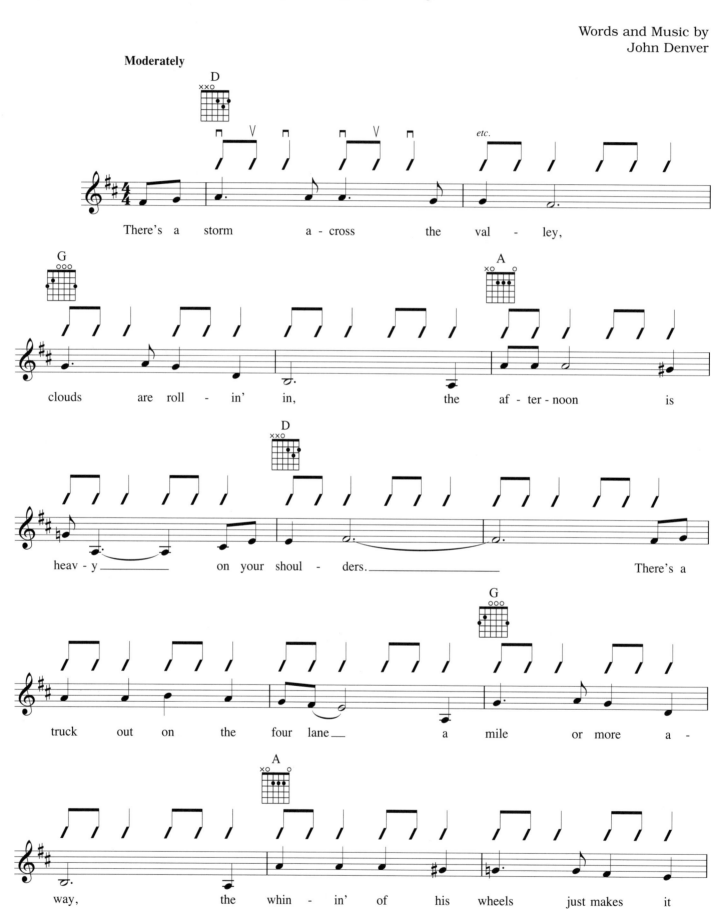

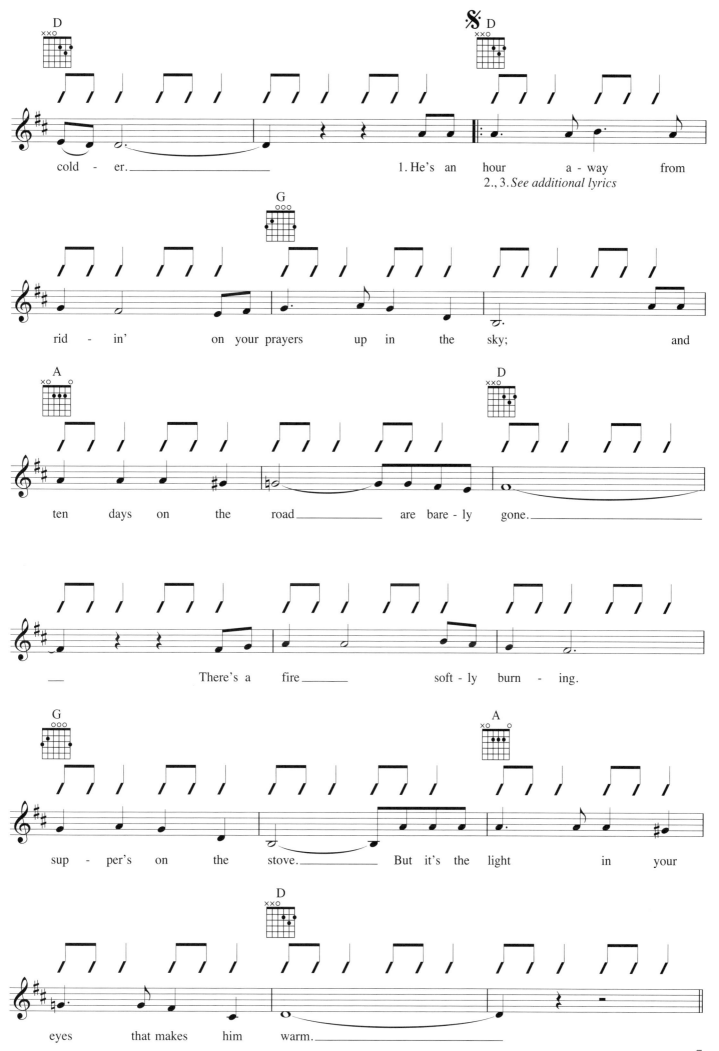

cold - er.

1. He's an hour a - way from
2., 3. See additional lyrics

rid - in' on your prayers up in the sky; and

ten days on the road are bare - ly gone.

There's a fire soft - ly burn - ing.

sup - per's on the stove. But it's the light in your

eyes that makes him warm.

87

Chorus

Hey, it's good to be back home a - gain; ____

____ some - times this old farm

feels like a long - lost friend. Yes 'n' hey, it's good to

1.

be back home a - gain. _____ 2. There's

2.

gain. _____ And oh, the time that

I can lay this tired old bod - y down and

feel   your   fin - gers   feath - er   soft   up - on   me.

___   The   kiss - es   that   I   live   for,   the

love   that lights   my   way,   the   hap - pi - ness   that

D.S. and fade on Chorus

liv - in'   with   you   brings   me.   3. It's   the

Additional Lyrics

2.   There's all the news to tell him: how'd you spend your time?
     And what's the latest thing the neighbors say?
     And your mother called last Friday; "Sunshine" made her cry,
     And you felt the baby move just yesterday. *(To Chorus)*

3.   It's the sweetest thing I know of, just spendin' time with you
     It's the little things that make a house a home.
     Like a fire softly burning and supper on the stove
     And the light in your eyes that makes me warm. *(To Chorus)*

INTRODUCING THE D MINOR CHORD

Dm

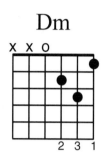

"America, the Beautiful"

Katharine Lee Bates, an instructor at Wellesley College in Massachusetts, wrote versions of the lyrics in 1893 after a trip to Pikes Peak in Colorado, and then again in 1904 and 1913. She did not associate the poem at the time with a particular melody, as far as we know, but it was eventually sung to the melody "Materna," which had been composed in 1882 by Samuel Ward.

Words by Katherine Lee Bates
Music by Samuel A. Ward

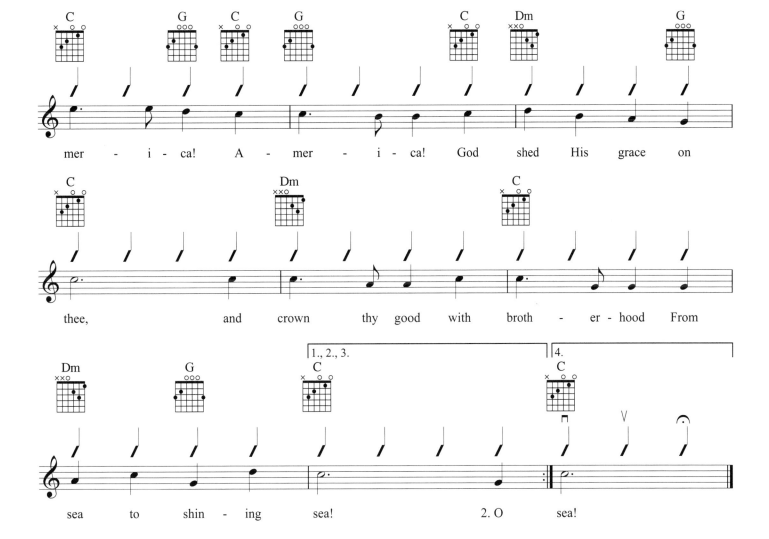

mer - i - ca! A - mer - i - ca! God shed His grace on

thee, and crown thy good with broth - er - hood From

1., 2., 3. | 4.

sea to shin - ing sea! 2. O sea!

Additional Lyrics

2. O beautiful for pilgrim feet
   Whose stern, impassioned stress
   A thoroughfare for freedom beat
   Across the wilderness!
   America! America!
   God mend thine every flaw,
   Confirm thy soul in self-control,
   Thy liberty in law!

3. O beautiful for patriot dream
   That sees beyond the years
   Thine alabaster cities gleam
   Undimmed by human tears!
   America! America!
   God shed his grace on thee,
   And crown thy good with brotherhood
   From sea to shining sea!

4. O beautiful for halcyon skies,
   For amber waves of grain,
   For purple mountain majesties
   Above the enameled plain!
   America! America!
   God shed his grace on thee,
   Till souls wax fair as earth and air
   And music-hearted sea!

"Greensleeves"

"Greensleeves" dates back to at least 1580. It is a love song—the story line regards an attempt to induce the wayward Lady Greensleeves to return to the love nest.

Sixteenth Century Traditional English

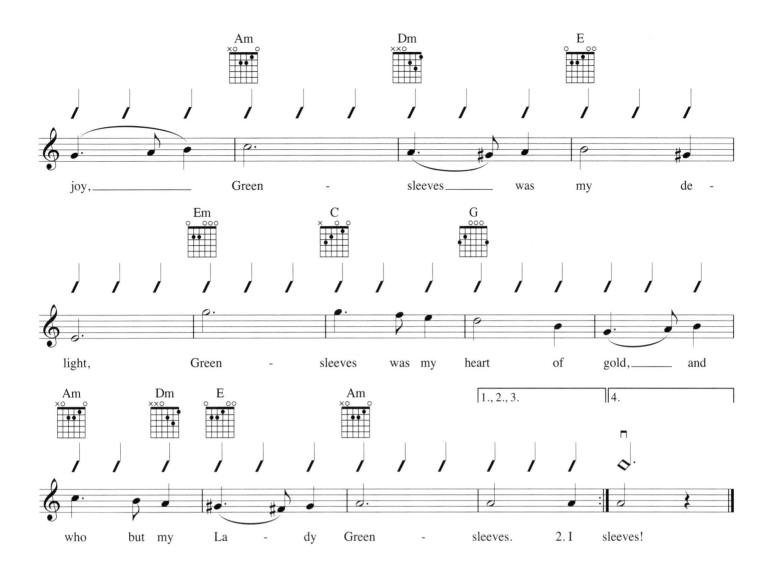

joy, _____ Green - sleeves _____ was my de -

light, Green - sleeves was my heart of gold, _____ and

who but my La - dy Green - sleeves. 2. I sleeves!

Additional Lyrics

2. I have been ready at your hand
    To grant whatever you would crave;
    I have both wagered life and land
    Your love and good will for to have *(To Chorus)*

3. I bought thee kerchers to thy head
    That were wrought fine and gallantly
    I kept thee both at board and bed
    Which cost my purse well favouredly. *(To Chorus)*

4. Greensleeves, now farewell! Adieu!
    God I pray to prosper thee,
    For I am still thy lover true,
    Come once again and love me. *(To Chorus)*

"Scarborough Fair"

This English folk song goes back to very early times, perhaps more than a thousand years. The Scarborough Fair was a huge 45-day trading event, starting August 15th of every year. People from all over England came to Scarborough to do their business.

The story line in the Verses (which here are more extensive than those used in the version by Simon and Garfunkel on their 1966 album, *Parsley, Sage, Rosemary and Thyme)* is that of a jilted lover trying to convince his opposite number to return to him. He assigns her all sorts of difficult tasks in order to demonstrate the difficulty of love. The herbs mentioned were all thought to cure stomach troubles and bitterness generally, so these would have facilitated the reunion.

A full and open sound works well in the accompaniment.

Traditional English

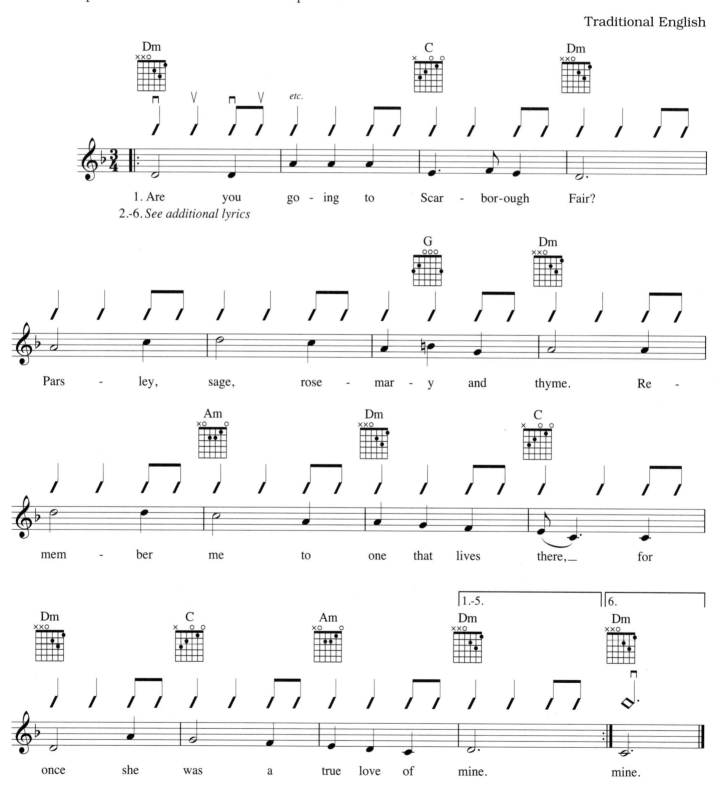

1. Are you go - ing to Scar - bor-ough Fair?
2.-6. *See additional lyrics*

Pars - ley, sage, rose - mar - y and thyme. Re -

mem - ber me to one that lives there,__ for

once she was a true love of mine. mine.

Additional Lyrics

2. Tell her to make me a cambric shirt,
   Parsley, sage, rosemary and thyme,
   Without no seam nor fine needle work,
   And then she'll be a true love of mine.

3. Tell her to find me an acre of land,
   Parsley, sage, rosemary and thyme
   Between the sea and over the sand,
   And then she'll be a true love of mine.

4. Tell her to reap it with a sickle of leather,
   Parsley, sage, rosemary and thyme,
   And gather it all in a bunch of heather,
   And then she'll be a true love of mine.

5. Love imposes impossible tasks,
   Parsley, sage, rosemary and thyme,
   Though not more than any heart asks,
   And I must know she's a true love of mine.

6. Dear, when thou has finished thy task,
   Parsley, sage, rosemary and thyme,
   Come to me, my hand for to ask,
   For thou then art a true love of mine.

■ *Congratulations!*

You've worked your way through the entire book and learned eight chords, several basic strumming patterns, and a truckload of songs in the process. Where can you go from here? You may wish to try lessons with a teacher or further books that can teach you the individual notes of the guitar, plus all sorts of nifty fingerpicking patterns and other techniques. By the way, you're now also well-equipped to tackle any number of "easy" guitar books that contain basic arrangements (not unlike those presented here with melodies, chords, and suggested strums) of all sorts of songs in all sorts of genres. The possibilities are limited only by your curiosity and your energy. Thanks for joining me on this little journey, and good luck in all of your musical endeavors!

■ ABOUT THE AUTHOR

Stephen Dydo has had a wide-ranging career. While pursuing a doctorate in music at Columbia University, he studied guitar with Ed Flower and guitar and lute with Pat O'Brien. At the same time that he was performing with various new music ensembles in New York, he wrote the arrangements for *The Norman Rockwell Family Songbook,* which was selected by the Book of the Month Club. His pieces for guitar and other instruments have been performed in the US and Europe by himself and other guitarists, such as Ben Verdery and Mike McCartney, to enthusiastic critical praise.

More Great Piano/Vocal Books from Cherry Lane

For a complete listing of Cherry Lane titles available, including contents listings, please visit our web site at
www.cherrylane.com

See your local music dealer or contact:

CHERRY LANE MUSIC COMPANY
6 East 32nd Street, New York, NY 10016

EXCLUSIVELY DISTRIBUTED BY

HAL•LEONARD® CORPORATION
7777 W. BLUEMOUND RD. P.O. BOX 13819 MILWAUKEE, WI 53213

Prices, contents and availability subject to change without notice.

0402